T0276582

PATHWORKING
the
TAROT

ABOUT THE AUTHOR

Leeza Robertson is the author of *Tarot Court Cards for Beginners* and *Tarot Reversals for Beginners*, and she's the creator of two tarot decks, the Mermaid Tarot and Animal Totem Tarot. Leeza spends her days dreaming up new tarot decks and exploring new ways to introduce more people to the world of tarot. When she doesn't have her nose in a book or her fingers running across a deck of cards, she runs an online Tarot Academy with her business partner Pamela Chen, which can be found online at Bit.ly/uftamagic.

LEEZA ROBERTSON

PATHWORKING
the
TAROT

SPIRITUAL GUIDANCE & PRACTICAL ADVICE FROM THE CARDS

LLEWELLYN PUBLICATIONS
Woodbury, Minnesota

Pathworking the Tarot: Spiritual Guidance & Practical Advice from the Cards ©
2019 by Leeza Robertson. All rights reserved. No part of this book may be used
or reproduced in any manner whatsoever, including internet usage, without written permission from Llewellyn Publications, except in the case of brief quotations
embodied in critical articles and reviews.

FIRST EDITION
First Printing, 2019

Book design: Samantha Penn
Cover design: Kevin Brown
Cover illustration: Christiane Beauregard / Lindgren & Smith
Editing: Annie Burdick

Llewellyn Publications is a registered trademark of Llewellyn Worldwide Ltd.

Library of Congress Cataloging-in-Publication Data (Pending)
ISBN: 978-0-7387-5787-2

Llewellyn Worldwide Ltd. does not participate in, endorse, or have any authority or responsibility concerning private business transactions between our authors
and the public.
    All mail addressed to the author is forwarded but the publisher cannot, unless
specifically instructed by the author, give out an address or phone number.
    Any internet references contained in this work are current at publication time,
but the publisher cannot guarantee that a specific location will continue to be
maintained. Please refer to the publisher's website for links to authors' websites and
other sources.

Llewellyn Publications
A Division of Llewellyn Worldwide Ltd.
2143 Wooddale Drive
Woodbury, MN 55125-2989
www.llewellyn.com

Printed in the United States of America

OTHER BOOKS BY LEEZA ROBERTSON

Tarot Court Cards for Beginners

Tarot Reversals for Beginners

Animal Totem Tarot

Mermaid Tarot

This book is for all those who have heard the call of tarot and decided to walk its path. This book was written for the tarot seeker, the tarot teacher, and the tarot reader. From beginner to lifelong acolyte, this book is for you.

CONTENTS

INTRODUCTION

IF YOU ARE NEW to tarot cards, then there is a good chance you are looking for ways to connect with the seventy-eight cards of your deck. If you are already knowledgeable in tarot, perhaps you are looking to deepen your relationship with the cards.

Tarot cards themselves can be confusing and overwhelming to novices. Each card is a complex construction of symbols and design features, geared to tell a very specific story. The version of that story will differ with each deck, as each deck creator will tell and retell that story in a unique and different way, emphasizing some elements and dismissing others. This means that the deck you hold in your hands right now is telling one version of a tarot story. Regardless of which deck you hold in your hands, you are looking at a unique interpretation of a story. I know from my own experience that each of my decks tells a story that is very heavily influenced by myself, my artist, the creative team, and the energy of the theme itself. This is one of the reasons I love creating tarot decks so much: so I can see how the story changes in its retelling based on who is involved in bringing that story into the world. In this respect, the very act of creating a tarot deck is also a form of pathwork or pathworking. It has specific rules and lessons, for both the deck creators and people just like you, who then pick the deck up and read with it. It has steps, processes, and a way of measuring progress. It is also an amazing personal and spiritual growth exercise. I am never the same after finishing a deck; I am forever changed, expanded, pushed, and pulled. My awareness is enhanced and my life deepened. Pathwork, just like tarot, is a story that is constantly told over and over again because it keeps changing and evolving. It is a walking meditation that guides you through the concerns, concepts, and philosophies that we call existence.

This book is broken up into five chapters. The cards themselves are broken up into three of those chapters, with the major arcana in chapter 2, the court cards in chapter 3, and the minor arcana, Aces through Tens, in chapter 4. In chapter 2, each card in the major arcana has its own pathwork exercises. However, I have set up the exercises differently in the minor arcana and court cards sections, and you will find only one set of pathwork exercises per number or court ranking. By this I mean there is only one set of exercises for the Pages, one set for the Knights, one set for the Queens, one set for the Kings. This format is replicated with the numbered cards, with one set for the Aces, one set for the Twos, and so on, all the way through the Tens. I have done this on purpose, as I see each element representing one part of a whole story for the numbered or court-ranking cards. In other words, all the Fives combined tell the complete story of the Fives, and all of the Knights combined tell the whole story of the Knight's experience. While this is not the only way you can pathwork with these cards, it is the way I have chosen to do it for the sake of this book. I have made sure that in no way is the pathwork experience diminished by doing it in this manner.

Chapter 1 is an introduction to pathwork and the exact processes I have chosen to use in this book, while chapter 5 wraps everything up and explains how to take this journey into your spreads and the spreads of your tarot clients.

My hope is that this book will inspire you to go further, deeper, and wider with your knowledge and understanding of how the cards influence your daily experience and assist you in expanding your spiritual being.

1

. . . .

WHAT IS PATHWORK?

PATHWORK IS A JOURNEY, in that it takes you from one point to another, but it is also an active exercise, not a passive practice. This journey can be physical in nature, meaning you literally travel through the steps one at a time, as you will find in some of the exercises in the wandering section of this book. But not everything about pathwork is physically active. Sometimes it is merely a matter of raising your level of awareness about who or what is around you as you move from one thought, feeling, or action to another. For example, you may find yourself standing next to the Magician or someone who acts like the Magician in your life, only to then find yourself in the company of someone who has similar qualities to the High Priestess. You might even find yourself needing to physically walk your way through the energy of one of the cards or, for something like the Five of Swords, walk it off! No matter how you end up pathworking with the cards of the tarot, you will find yourself engaging with their lessons and messages more actively, which means you have to be willing to deal with what comes up while you take this journey. This is where the messy nature of pathworking comes in: dealing with the emotional stuff. Spiritual expansion is messy; it pushes your buttons and makes you uncomfortable. If you don't feel any of these things, you are not going deep enough. Pathwork will push and trigger those of you who like to dwell on the surface of your emotions. You can only ever observe from the surface—pathwork means diving in, breaking the surface, and getting yourself wet with emotional fluids. If something makes you feel comfortable, it is not going to push you to grow. Comfort is for resting, stopping, and saying "I am good where I am." It is perfectly okay for people to crave comfort; I just advise you not to allow it to make you stagnant, as that is when life's problems arise.

For this book I have come up with three different ways to pathwork with your tarot cards, which I use myself and use with my clients. They are not overly complex nor are they rigid in structure, and they have a tendency to overlap. This is something else one learns through pathwork—things are more fluid and more connected than we like to admit. The lines between exercises and labels will at times seem tenuous at best, but just flow with them anyway. The differences may be more suggestive than you are actually giving them credit for. Although I have not really set up the book to be read in a specific way, you will find suggestions on how to approach each part of the tarot deck; for example, with the suits, Aces through Tens work in a sequence. You can choose to work with just all the intentional exercises for your cards if it seems more fitting for your readings, or you could work with each exercise from top to bottom. But there are no real hard and fast rules here. Use the book intuitively. Allow the exercises to guide you and help deepen your understanding of the cards, your spreads, and your work with tarot. The three pathworking exercises I want to introduce you to are as follows.

1. Intentional

Each card of the tarot has a very specific story, theme, or set of lessons and challenges it presents. With intentional pathwork, you may need to deliberately select your card and your journey based on the theme, lesson, or challenge you wish to work with, work through, or deepen. This means going into your deck and actively choosing a card you wish to pathwork with. Let's say you want to attract more money into your life or you want to attract a new job or get your energy aligned with that big promotion that may be coming up. You should pull out your deck and find the card that vibrates to the energy you wish to achieve.

For these work and money queries, it might be the Nine of Pentacles or the Queen of Pentacles. The Nine of Pentacles may radiate the feeling of being financially secure and abundant, which is how you want to feel so you can attract even more of that energy. Also helpful, the Queen of Pentacles may make you feel in control, empowered, and viewed as someone of importance.

Each of the cards in your deck offers you a journey, one that will move you into the vibration you need to manifest your goal. Do you see how you deliberately choose the card and the energy you wanted to work with? This is, in essence, how the intentional exercises work in this book. But it is not the only way, and you will see some of the intentional exercises can be just as intuitive as the intuitive exercises. This is the nature of pathwork: things merge and blend; sometimes the boundaries aren't as clear as you would like them to be.

2. Intuitive

In the intuitive exercises, you may find yourself prompted to release what you think you need to know and just let the card tell you. This is more like channeling the card, listening to it speak to you, and allowing it to guide you on your journey without any nudging from your ego mind. This process opens up possibilities for a card that you would never receive another way. Oftentimes we can get fixated on what a card means or how it has to be interpreted, but this way you take all of your preconceived ideas and throw them out the window.

How you go about selecting your card intuitively will depend on you, although I do have instructions in most of the intuitive sections. You can shuffle your deck, hold it to your heart with your question or intention in your mind, then just split your deck, taking whatever card happens to be on top. Or you can shuffle, cut with your cards facedown, and draw the card from the top of the deck. Or you can choose not to shuffle them at all, fan them out facedown, and run a pendulum over them to see which card is speaking the loudest in answer to your question.

This section is really about letting go—stop trying to force or control an outcome and instead allow the outcome to flow to you. Most tarot readers already work with this intuitive approach when they do a reading anyway, so this part of the pathwork process should come easy enough to most of you reading this book. But again, this is not the only way the exercises in this section are presented. So do not balk if you come across one that looks more intentional than intuitive.

3. Wandering

Wandering uses a little of the first method's intention, a dash of the second method's intuition, and a lot of action. The wandering technique is really more about how well you know your mind and what level of control you have over it. It is easier to focus on something by setting an intention, and it is even pretty easy to open up to a concept, idea, or problem and see what intuitive hit you might get. But to allow yourself to wander and explore with no real destination—that's where the deep digging really happens. I discovered this technique during my own meditation process, as I observed how one thing would trigger something else and send me in a totally different direction, until that also triggered something else, and I would ping off again. I learn more about who I am while wandering, though it is not for everyone.

So, what is wandering in the scheme of this book and in the process of pathwork? Wandering is a twofold active process, as it can be done in the mind or through the body. You can take a thought for a walk inside your head, or you can walk it out in the world around you. I am a walker; I live for my morning walks and they are very much a part of my healing and mediation practice, as they literally move energy in, around, and through my physical body. Sometimes this is exactly what a thought, problem, or question needs to do as well. It needs to be moved physically. It needs to be allowed space and opportunity to move unhindered. This is what the prompts in the wandering sections of the cards will do for you. Sometimes they will involve a physical wandering and you will be asked to move your physical body; other times it might just be mental wandering to see where a thought, idea, or problem takes you. This is probably the section that may give some of you the most difficulty, as I am not sure how many of you have ever taken a tarot card for a walk. Again, this section is about flow, about letting go and learning how to engage with your cards in a new and deeper way. There is no wrong or right way to do it, so just let the prompts in this book guide you.

Now you have the framework, or at least a rough idea of pathwork and the methods used here in the cards sections of this book. Don't worry if this still all sounds like an alien language. It will come together as you do the exercises for each of the cards. New concepts take time, and they need to be practiced over and over again. This is another great thing about the pathwork process: it is repetitious. I would suggest you just work with one card a week to begin. Sit with the exercises for the card and see how each of them plays out in your daily life or watch to see if they change your point of perception. Maybe you want to work with the suit of wands and you choose to just go through the intuitive exercises until you have a better understanding of the suit on an intuitive level. Or maybe the idea of taking the majors for a walk really appeals to you, so you spend the next twenty-two days doing a wandering challenge with your twenty-two major arcana cards. However you decide to launch into this book will be the right way for you. My only suggestion would be to initially only work with one card per day until you get the hang of the process. There is information in chapter 5 on how to take this one step further and bring the pathwork process into your spreads.

I also strongly recommend keeping a separate journal to keep your pathworking notes. It's important to note that journal writing and pathworking are not the same. They can share similar elements, but they are very different. They do, however, go together like ice cream and chocolate. We have already established that pathwork can be messy; it brings stuff up from the murky emotional waters and you may find you need extra time to work through what the pathwork process pushes to the surface. This is where your journal will come in. In many respects, the pathwork process triggers the journal process. What you feel, see, and experience on your pathwork journey will ultimately trigger issues, points of healing, and other sore spots that you may wish to keep a record of. The deeper you pathwork with your cards, the more you may find yourself reaching for your journal. To assist you in knowing how to best use a journal through this specific process, I have included journal tips and prompts within the exercises, just so you don't get confused along the way. But please, don't let my prompts be the only things to get you to your journal. Use your journal as a companion buddy to your pathwork, reach for it whenever you feel it necessary, and don't use it if you don't feel it is applicable to the information or energy you engage in with a specific exercise or card.

Choosing Your Pathwork Deck

Although technically any tarot deck will do for this sort of work, you may want to either go through your deck collection to find a deck that fits this sort of work, or buy a new deck. I myself have decks that I don't read from but I do use for pathwork, spellwork, and journal work. These decks tend to have less traditional images and offer space for the imagination to take over. A couple of decks I enjoy using for this sort of work are the Gaian Tarot, the Raven's Prophecy Tarot, and the Paulina Tarot. These decks are visually intriguing beyond their assigned tarot meaning. They offer a visual feast and let one get lost in the image itself. You will need to find one or two decks that do that for you, ones that just visually move you and draw you into the scene. What works for me more than likely won't work for you, as each of us has our own level of visual sensitivity. Some people prefer softer images with more pastel colors, some like darker colors with high fantasy art, and others might want something somewhere in between. Only you will know what images you are looking for in a deck of cards. Most of you will more than likely already know which deck in your collection ticks all the boxes for you and offers itself intuitively to the pathwork process. If you are fairly new to tarot or don't have a very extensive collection of decks, I encourage you to seek out a deck just for this work. Find groups on Facebook or Instagram where you might be able to trade decks, or take yourself shopping and find the perfect deck for your pathwork journey. It might even take you a while to settle into a deck. Just set your intention for the most aligned deck, see it arriving to you in the most perfect of circumstances, and before you know it you will have your very own pathwork tarot deck added to your collection.

Okay, pick a deck of cards and let's jump in!

2

THE MAJOR ARCANA

THE CARDS OF THE major arcana follow a very unique sequence. They act somewhat like steps, each one leading on to the next, adding and building one's skill set and one's understanding of their place and purpose in the world. Yet life very rarely runs in the sequential order the major arcana offers up, so why is it important that we engage with the cards as if it does? Regardless of how you make your way through the twenty-two cards of the major arcana, you cannot escape the fact that they all have an influence on one another. There is a reason Death, Temperance, and the Devil are found hanging out together, just like the Star, Moon, and Sun. There is a story being told throughout these twenty-two cards and each step is a chapter in that story, carrying on from the chapter before it and paving the way for the chapter after it. The only card of the majors that does not seem to follow this rule is the Fool. The

Fool seems separate from the rest, not really belonging to any one chapter, but rather acting as the main character that moves through the story, steps, and sequence of the remaining twenty-one cards. The Fool does this at their own pace, in their own time and their own way. The Fool does not seem bound to the same sort of rules the other twenty-one cards are bound to, which makes your relationship with the Fool that much more important. As you make your way through this chapter and land on each of the twenty-two steps, you will have to decide if you are the Fool, or if the Fool is someone outside of yourself that you are observing having this journey through the other major arcana cards. This decision will have an impact on how you, in turn, experience the other twenty-one cards. You will either see them as something that is happening to you or something that is happening outside of you that you observe but do not partake in. I should point out that there is no wrong or right way to engage with the twenty-two cards of the major arcana; just know that they are a system, a series of steps that are there to guide you in whatever way you personally feel is right for you. Nothing more, nothing less.

0. THE FOOL

The Fool is the start of a journey, be it through the remaining twenty-one cards of the major arcana or some other journey in your current life. The Fool embodies elements of spontaneity, innocence, faith, risk, and courage. The Fool is by no means a passive card; it is action-oriented, for you cannot begin anything without movement. However, there is also something beautifully still and calm about the energy of the Fool, for they have not yet learned how to fear the world around them. The Fool does not seem to be filled with the trepidation and doubts most seasoned travelers have. This innocence means the mind is calm and the heart is wide open. The mind is not racing to all the things that could go wrong, but instead is wrapped up in the heart's song of what could actually go right. This is echoed by the number that the Fool is assigned—zero, full of untapped potential but also carrying nothing at all. This idea or concept that we can be filled to the brim with potential in all of its forms but empty at the same time is at the very heart of the meditation process. To be empty of fear, doubt, and ego and full of the divine or universal spark is what most meditators are striving for. In the Fool card, this state of being is as natural as breathing. There is no need to seek this feeling, for it is just by being the Fool that it is attained. This is something to ponder further as you make your way through the pathworking exercises.

PATHWORK

Intentional

For this exercise, bring to mind the last time you acted in a spontaneous or impulsive way. Relax into the thought and bring the scene to the forefront of your mind. See it as if it were a snapshot in your mind's eye. Taking another nice deep breath, connect with how you felt in the moment you decided to let your hair down, be a little reckless, and act without thinking. Don't allow your mind to wander into analysis. You are the observer while you are undertaking this pathwork exercise, and you can do all the examination you want in your journal later. Right now just focus on how you felt while taking that leap. Don't judge the feeling; just let it bubble up to the surface. Taking another deep breath, fast forward to the next day, the day after you were spontaneous or impulsive. Did you still feel good about how you acted, or did you wake up with buyer's remorse? Again, do not spend a lot of time analyzing how you felt, just observe. Take another deep breath, then exhale deeply, letting it all go, as if you were pushing the air all the way down to and through your feet. Do this one more time to truly disconnect from the energy of the Fool and your journey.

If you notice that you had a very positive reaction to your walk in the wild with the energy of the Fool, amplify it, take note of it, and journal about it. If you notice that you felt regret or shame, just take note of it and write about it after you have finished this exercise. Get your journal and start writing about your findings, keeping the Fool card with you at all times while you do the journal work.

Intuitive

For this exercise, you are going to talk your way through the Fool card. In other words, you are going to tell the story of the card as if you are the Fool. If you feel you need to record your ramblings, grab your phone and record them. I like to hook up my headset to my laptop and start my talk-to-text function, so that I can get a written account of my session with the Fool card. If you don't feel comfortable recording your journey, that is fine; you don't have to do it, but it is extremely helpful.

Stare into your card and get a feel for the environment and landscape the Fool finds themselves in. Is your Fool on the edge of a cliff? If so, does being that close to the edge freak you out? Describe the scene around you, even the weather. Don't forget to mention if you have an animal totem companion and what you have in your knapsack. You might want to start this exercise by saying something along the lines of "I am the Fool who ..."

Let me give you a quick example using the Fool card from the Animal Totem Tarot: "I am the Fool who carries more than I need.

I am the Fool who jumps into adventure without wearing sunscreen. I am the Fool who sees the clear blue skies and runs to come out and play."

Okay, now it's your turn. *I am the fool who…*

Wandering

There is a Fool in all of us. We are all prone to wander through our lives in the Fool's shoes at some point. You know only too well what it is like to get caught up in the moment of something and forget about everything else. Time, food, money, your physical body… they all fade away when you find yourself having a Fool moment experience. For this exercise, see if you can tap into one of those moments today. See if you can identify when everything around you just fades out and you lose all track of time. Learning to tap into these moments is one of the first steps to finding the gaps in your physical experience and allowing your soul to take over. This gap moves you into a vibrational experience, a more transcended experience. The Fool is very much the first step to self-actualization. But just for today, see if you can identify the gap, the Fool moment.

1. THE MAGICIAN

The number one card in the major arcana is the Magician, the card of the self-sufficient, fully equipped, magical creator. This card deals with elements of purpose, destiny, divine gifts, and, of course, magic. The Magician brings all the elements of the tarot together in one place: earth, air, fire, and water—all of the elements needed to create, sustain, and destroy life. That's a lot to deal with in one card. The Magician is the next step up from the Fool, for here we see our Fool has learned some new tricks and is discovering how to tap into the energy of possibility and potential that was surrounding them in the previous card. I guess we could say that here in the Magician, the Fool has unlocked their talents and is now sorting through them to see which ones they might want to develop further as they continue their journey through the tarot world.

So what skills and talents are on offer here? I do believe this is an important element of the Magician card, for we won't all have the same skills, possibilities, or magic at our disposal. We each have different gifts or talents that will be available for us to explore, foster, and grow, and it is up to us to determine what they are. So look at your Magician card carefully, really connect with the image, and allow yourself to be open to seeing what gifts you are meant to explore. Your magic is unique and only you can unlock its true potential, so take your time as you step into the shoes of the Magician.

PATHWORK

Intentional

Do you believe you are the creator of your own destiny, or do you believe that your life is out of your hands? These questions are fundamental to the Magician card. For the purpose of this exercise, let's say you believe you are the creator of your life. Let's say you consider this a powerful, self-affirming card and one that helps you focus on your divine gifts to create a life of joy, wealth, health, and love. Close your eyes and think about the last time you and you alone manifested something you really wanted into your life. Think about the people, conditions, and actions you had to meet and manage to pull it all off. Bring it all into your mind's eye and hold that image. How does this image make you feel? What mindset did you have at the time this manifestation happened? Take nice deep breaths as you sit with this image and the feelings it bubbles up. Magnify this image, brighten it, make it as vibrant as possible, and affirm: "I see you, I remember you, I live you in every moment."

Slowly release the image and bring your awareness back to the room. This is a way of tapping into your unique magic, a way for you to see how your gifts and talents come together to create just for you. Remember not to judge any of this—just allow yourself to relive the moment and observe, and please leave comparison at the door.

Intuitive

Hold your Magician card out in front of you and just start talking your way through it as if you were the Magician. Start in the same way we did back in the Fool, only this time start with something along the lines of "I am the Magician who..."

Let me give you an example: "I am the Magician who uses my gifts to benefit not only myself but all those around me. I am the Magician who knows how to play to my gifts and strengths. I am the Magician who is always in the right place at the right time with the right magical tool." I think you get the idea. The purpose of this exercise is to get you comfortable with your magic, with your special and unique gift and power. Do the speaking exercise out loud until you run out of things to say.

Wandering

This is an exercise in channeling your cards. By making a psychic link between the figure in the card and yourself, you are opening the door for a direct dialogue. Don't worry if you only get a couple of words or just a sentence. The more you do this sort of exercise the stronger the connection becomes.

Place your Magician card in front of you, either on a table or desk. Pick up a pen and some paper. Gaze at the card and allow your eyes to wander over it, soaking in the image, the colors, and the design. If possible, stare into the eyes of the Magician. Pick up your pen and start writing whatever pops into your head. Just write for five to ten minutes, keeping your gaze on the Magician and never breaking your connection until you feel you are done and have written all you can. Even if you only get one sentence or a handful of random words, you have done well.

2. THE HIGH PRIESTESS

The High Priestess is a bit of a mysterious card. The Priestess is considered high in stature, is elite in her education, and is the keeper of sacred knowledge. In more traditional decks she is also the protector and gatekeeper of the higher realms of wisdom and self-realization. However, she gives no clues whatsoever as to what she is actually protecting and whom she is protecting it from, though to look at a traditional version of this card, you would think it was whoever happened to cross her path. She is in many respects a high-ranking female guru, and all who come before her usually come with a question.

So what is yours? What answers do you seek at the feet of the High Priestess? What knowledge are you hoping she will bestow upon you, and in all honesty, do you think you are worthy? I guess you are about to find out. Before you walk the path with the High Priestess you must first consider what it is you wish for her to tell you. Like all great spiritual gurus, she won't just open up and tell you everything she knows. Instead, she will only offer that which she feels you need, and even that isn't definite. So, what is the one most pressing issue or concern you have right now in your life? You only get one question per visit, so make it a good one. Once you have decided what your question will be, think about what you are willing to offer her as a gift, as you must first give an offering in honor of the Priestess before you expect anything in return. Now that you have both your gift and your question, you are ready to set yourself on the path to the High Priestess.

PATHWORK

Intentional

In this exercise you are going to journey to the temple of the High Priestess. Pull the High Priestess card from your deck and place it somewhere you can see it and use it as a point of focus for your journey. Get comfortable, relax, and remember to breathe. Gaze at your card and focus on the temple, seeing yourself walking the path that leads to where your High Priestess is seated. Do your best to relax into the scene that unfolds before you, knowing that you can close your eyes at any time to zero in on your surroundings or focus your mental energy. As you walk the path to the temple, take notice of what surrounds it; notice whether there are people and animals or if the landscape looks barren or isolated.

Keep walking until you find yourself at the door to the temple. Remember, you need to bring the High Priestess a gift, something you will give her in exchange for the information you seek from her. So make sure you have it ready as you knock and wait patiently for the guard. Hand your gift to the guard and wait to be granted permission inside. Relax even more and just allow the rest of the journey to unfold. Do not push it, force it, or reject it. If the guard allows you access, enter the temple and sit with the High Priestess. Allow your experience with her to unfold as it needs to.

If you are not allowed in, that means the High Priestess believes that the answer you seek is already in your possession, so just take a moment to yourself outside the temple and look at whether you are holding anything in your hands or find something under your foot.

When you feel your time is done at the temple, take some nice deep breaths and bring yourself back to your body and back to the space you are sitting in. Now that the journey is over, you are free to write about this encounter in your journal.

Intuitive

The High Priestess is an intuitive card. Connected to the Moon, the High Priestess wants you to consider that what you seek you already know. For this exercise, she wants you to tap into your own inner knowing and your own High Priestess and listen. Put your High Priestess card somewhere you can see it, then pick up a pen and some paper or open your laptop and create a new document.

Ask a question out loud to the High Priestess and then just write down whatever you hear. You might hear it just inside your head or maybe a song or tune will float through your window at that exact moment. Keep the question in your mind, and keep your ears open. Do this for about two to four minutes. Set a timer if it helps you stay focused. When your time is up, read what you have in front of you. It may not be the exact answer you were hoping for, but it will be a mighty fine place to start. If you want to take this exercise one step further, take your findings to your journal.

Wandering

Would you know how to identify the High Priestess if you bumped into her on the street? I ask this because this archetype is a bit of a chameleon. Just like her counterpart, the Moon, the High Priestess can take on more than one face or phase. For this exercise, see if you can identify the High Priestess in your life. See if you can find her in your family, at your place of employment, and even in your home. Maybe the High Priestess is you. This archetype is hard to find in the wild, as sometimes she is one of the Queens, sometimes she is one of the Knights, sometimes she can even be one of the Pages. This exercise will help you learn to identify people who seem to have one foot in the physical world but their head in the spiritual realm. Your teachers, mentors, and spiritual wisdom-keepers never quite look the way you expect them to, so pay very close attention. Good luck, and don't be surprised if you have to spend quite a bit of time playing hide and seek with the High Priestess.

3. THE EMPRESS

The great mother of the deck is the embodiment of Venus, the Goddess of Love. She is nurturing, giving, and constantly creating. Yet she is more than just a woman who always seems barefoot and pregnant. The whole idea of pregnancy and birth is debated within the energy of this card, along with the idea of what we define as a mother. Not every woman gives literal birth to another life, and men cannot do it at all; yet both are just as much a part of the Empress as those women who can, and do, bring physical new life into the world. It is within the Empress that we start to see that maybe the way we have defined the world is not as concrete as we first thought. It is under the loving gaze of the Empress that we start to think about identity, purpose, and how we wish to engage in the material world of physicality. For if the Empress can be fluid in self-identification, perhaps so can we. It is here with the Empress that we start to learn that gender is not identity and identity is not gender. This idea will be explored even further throughout the court cards.

The Empress's deep connection to the earth means she can teach you how to birth your ideas into the material world; however, she will be brutally honest about the level of sacrifice you will have to make in order to create all that you want and desire. The Empress knows only too well about processes and cycles. She understands there are no shortcuts or overnight successes. If you are willing to walk the path of creation with her, she will be more than eager to share some of her tips and tricks along the way, but be forewarned, her advice is not for the faint-hearted.

PATHWORK

Intentional

The Empress is our first lesson in process, stages, and cycles. In order to create something, it must first be conceived, then go through a gestational process, and then be birthed into the world. After it is born, the hard work begins. But for now, let's focus on gestation. In today's instant gratification world, waiting for things to happen can seem like a cruel form of torture. But the Empress knows that in order for things to be birthed in the right way at the right time, there needs to be a specific gestational period.

As you think about projects, ideas, or relationships you seem to be waiting on, take a nice deep breath. Just relax and breathe out any and all tension you have created around the idea of having to wait. Focus on exhaling the tension and anxiety while you inhale the calming and more nurturing energy of the Empress. Feel the unconditional love she has for you and your creations. Let it wash over your body. As you breathe in the energy of the Empress and exhale the tension, bring to your mind's eye the end result you are rushing so hard to get to. Make this image as sharp and bright as you can. Allow the energy from the Empress to seep into this end result image you are focusing on and see how it makes you feel. Sink into the visual representation of seeing your goal achieved.

Notice who is there with you. Notice what sort of environment you are in.

As you make this image larger, brighter, and more lifelike, notice any and all tension or anxiety that creeps into your body. Just keep breathing it out, and do not release your primary focus from your vision. As you take in your achievement and the amazing feelings this achievement gives you, ask yourself if you are willing to compromise any of this. How it looks, how it feels, and who is there with you are all products of your goal coming together in divine time, and divine time is the Empress's domain. This vision is the end result of the perfect gestational period. Allow that to sink in, and then when you are ready, take three nice, long, deep breaths in through the nose and out through your mouth, and just let the image fade away. Release it with the knowledge that it is on its way to you. Let go of your need to control when it shows up, and instead put it in the hands of the Empress. Allow her to guide it through its divine gestational period, knowing she will be more than willing to give it back to you once it is time for you to birth it into the world. Relax, roll out your shoulders, take the Empress card out of your deck, and place her either on your altar or beside your bed. Leave her there for the next three days. Each morning and evening, look at your card and say "Thank you."

Intuitive

For this journey, take your Empress card out of your deck and put her somewhere you can see her. Next, open up your yearly planner or digital calendar. Take a deep breath and ask the Empress to give you a date of expectancy. You can word this any way you want. You may ask her for a due date for your goal or maybe a deadline for phase one of a longer project. Just find a way to ask, then close your eyes and let the date come to you. No matter what date it is, put it in your calendar. This may seem a little out there, but I have learned over the years that the Empress is never wrong with her timing. Even when I am on a contractual deadline, I ask the Empress for a due date, and without fail she gives it to me. It is always right every single time, without exception. Once you have your date marked you can relax into that fact and know that you now have a solid time frame to work with, meaning you now know just how long your gestational period will be.

Wandering

If you were to take the Empress for a walk, where would you take her and why? Think about the fact that she is heavily pregnant; what would you need to do to accommodate her? Take into consideration that her connection to Venus means she has a preference for beauty. And last but not least, consider the fact that she is used to getting her own way. Take this all into consideration before you plan your outing. Now, start making a list of all the places you want to take the Empress. Make bullet points as to why you think the Empress would enjoy herself at these places, and consider if you yourself would also enjoy them. You just never know; planning a trip for the Empress may turn into a trip-planning event for yourself!

4. THE EMPEROR

Have you ever imagined what it would be like to build your own world? To have a world that was in alignment with your own personal beliefs, thoughts, and feelings? Can you even see what sort of people would live there and how the structure of the society would work? It is not easy thinking about having massive numbers of people in your care. It is not easy to set the rules and regulations that hundreds, thousands, or millions would have to live their lives by. Yet this is exactly what the Emperor does. He is law, he is structure, he is the creator of his own Empire, the builder of his own world. It is easy for us to think we know all the answers to solve the world's problems, but the truth is that no one does. Humans as a collective are messy, complex, and often paradoxical. To build an empire you have to think about the many and live with the few that do not agree with you. To create a world means establishing one set of ideals, beliefs, and biases and expecting everyone else to follow them. The job of the Emperor is a difficult and unrewarding one. Maybe that is why from time to time he locks himself away and only bothers to indulge his own needs and wants. All good leaders should have "me time"; however, they also know this is not something they can do forever.

The Emperor in the tarot represents the divine masculine, the energy that works harmoniously alongside the divine feminine. You can tell when the divine masculine is out of alignment, because it is not sharing the spotlight with its female consort. In order for any world to be fair and balanced, the divine gendered energies must be on equal footing. The Emperor knows this, which is why he is more than happy for the Empress to come before him in the first row of the major arcana. He doesn't need to upstage or outshine anyone, as he has too many other things on his mind, and without the help of the Empress, nothing he builds will grow. This is important when you start your pathwork journey with the Emperor, for oftentimes people forget that the Emperor doesn't create worlds on his own. He is not a singular entity as such; he is part of the whole, and without the other pieces there would be no need for any of the things he can build, create, or bring together. The foundation he forges needs others to engage with it, support it, nourish it, and help it expand.

PATHWORK

Intentional

When it is time to get serious and get our hands dirty, it is time to pull the Emperor from our decks and start to work alongside this builder of dreams deliberately and with purpose. Emperor isn't just a ruler and commander in chief, he is also a creator; he constructs things, often with his own two hands. This is the energy you will need when you want to manifest something from your dreams into your physical experience. This simple mantra-style spell will help you channel your inner Emperor and get you focused on building your own empire.

Go ahead and remove your Emperor card from your deck. Put it either on your altar space or somewhere it won't be disturbed for the next twenty-four hours. You can pair your card with crystals, herbs, or even building tools. Write out a small mantra on a piece of paper, something along the lines of "I call on my inner Emperor to show me what tools I need to pick up to assist me in building the life of my dreams," or "Dear Emperor, show my how I can lead by example so I can best serve those around me." You will know what it is you want your Emperor to assist you with.

Once you have your card on your altar and your mantra written, take a nice relaxing breath, light a candle or some incense, and recite your mantra three times. Sit silently for a couple of minutes and then finish up by saying, "Thank you for helping me construct the life of my dreams."

And that's it. You can repeat this over the next few days if you feel called to.

Intuitive

In my book *Tarot Court Cards for Beginners* I talked about how each of the four Kings could be seen to show different aspects of the Emperor himself. For example, the King of Cups is a heart-based leader, the King of Swords is a thought leader, the King of Wands is a creative leader, and the King of Pentacles is an investment leader. All four show totally different ways to lead, build, and govern.

In this exercise, I want you to pull out your Emperor card, your four Kings, and your four Queens. Place the Emperor faceup so you can see him staring back at you. Gather up your Kings and Queens, keeping them facedown, and give them a little shuffle. Fan them out and pick two cards, card one being your main leadership influence and card two your secondary leadership energy. Card one indicates how the outside world sees you and card two shows how you see yourself. Did you turn over cards that surprise you or are your results no surprise at all? Pick up your journal and write about the differences between how the world sees you and how you see yourself. Think about whether or not you are comfortable with the differences or if it is something you would like to work on. The more you get to know these two cards, the more you will be able to manifest, serve, and engage with those around you.

Wandering

Do you want to walk in the Emperor's shoes? Do you want to see how glamorous it is to have the world at your feet? I know there are times I do. I want to sit on that throne, be the one giving orders, and have others look up to me with deep respect and trust in their eyes. I want to know what it feels like to have world-changing power at my fingertips. If you struggle with confidence of any kind, this exercise is a good one to practice on a regular basis. Getting into that *feeling* place of the Emperor will help you tremendously. All you have to do is immerse yourself in your Emperor card, see yourself merging with the image on the card, and slowly allow yourself to observe from behind the Emperor's eyes. You may be brave enough to become the Emperor yourself, or you might be able to take a backseat and observe the Emperor's actions, decision-making, and strength. How you approach your wandering is entirely up to you. The braver you get, the more you might find yourself becoming more Emperor and less observer. Just take your time and allow the feeling to build at your pace.

5. THE HIEROPHANT

How you relate to this card really does say a lot about how you view religion and spirituality in general. I know some people tend to view this card as limiting, a reminder of the overreach of traditional religious institutions and a visual representation of all their rules and regulations. I understand how easy it is to get fixated on this view of the Hierophant, especially considering that the church was pretty connected to this card in the fifteenth century, with many decks labeling this card as the Pope. But don't forget that right alongside the Pope was the female Pope, also known as the High Priestess. It was a different time with different values and traditions. I know others who see the Hierophant as a teacher, storyteller, wise wisdom-keeper, and the one who passes knowledge, medicine, and wisdom from one generation to another. There are others who see him as a spiritual guide, someone who helps you along the path to enlightenment and self-actualization. All of these are religious and spiritual in nature, but how you feel about each manifestation of the Hierophant will have a very real impact on how you work with the energy of this card, and what you will or will not allow it to teach you.

For the sake of this book and your pathworking experience, we are going to use the Hierophant in all of his forms. He is going to be Pope, priest, monk, wisdom-keeper, storyteller, and all-around guru. We are also going to see him as a representation of the paradox that expansion can only happen through limitation. Love him or hate him, the Hierophant has an awful lot to teach you about who you are, why you are here, and how you can stay focused on your life path. As with all good spiritual mentors, you will find yourself both running from him and running toward him, until you settle into the lessons and wisdom he has for you. Working with a spiritual teacher is hard for many reasons, and a lot of people have had bad experiences in the past that now darken the idea of trying again.

Just keep in mind that picking a spiritual teacher or finding the Hierophant that is right for you may take some time. It might also push you to drop some of your own preconceived ideas about what a spiritual teacher should and should not be like. Find teachers who are joyful, abundant, authentic, believe in integrity, and above all are loved and give love back willingly. In other words, don't pick an asshat. This is one of the ways working with the Hierophant can be beneficial, as he holds the space for you to explore your options. He creates a place for you to consider what it is you truly want from a spiritual path. He is not interested in what he can get out of you, only what you can find out about yourself and your place in the larger vibrational web of the universe.

PATHWORK

Intentional

Who are your spiritual mentors and why do you look up to them? During this pathwork exercise, select one of your spiritual teachers or someone you wish to emulate. It doesn't really have to be someone who walks a spiritual path, just someone you respect, listen to, and model your life after. Sit in silent, reflective meditation and contemplate how this person or their words or their music or their beliefs have benefited you. View all the ways this person has made your life better, more joyful, or more grounded. Allow these feelings to just bubble up and roll through you. Feel them as they rise and fall. Notice any sensations as these feelings, thoughts, and memories wash over you. Remember to breathe as you continue to focus on these sensations. Once you have reflected as much as possible, visualize yourself sending your teacher, mentor, or role model waves of gratitude. See this gratitude pour from your heart center and out into the world, eventually falling down on your target like gentle spring rain. Notice if your gratitude is a specific color. Also notice how your body feels as it sends out these pulse-like waves of gratitude and affection. Relax, breathe, and when you feel finished, allow yourself a few moments to settle back into the here and now. If this person has had a very large impact on your life, you could make this a monthly practice. Sending their vibrational bodies gratitude makes them able to continue their work and help others. Your small reflective meditation can be a part of that bigger vibrational web.

Intuitive

Remove your Hierophant card from your deck and place it in front of you. Shuffle your remaining cards, and while you do so, ask your Hierophant what spiritual lesson he has for you today. When you feel ready, go ahead and select a card, then place it faceup next to your Hierophant card. So, what does your spiritual mentor want you to know today? What lesson does he want you to learn? Can you think of why this particular lesson may be popping up now? Sit with both of these cards for a while, keeping your gaze on them, while you contemplate the card you have drawn. When you feel ready, pick up your journal and let your mind rattle off anything and everything that has pushed itself to the forefront of your awareness. Save it and read it tomorrow. Space often gives us even more perspective.

Wandering

Once upon a time if one wanted to have a spiritual experience, one had to either renounce all that they owned and all of their labels, and join a wandering band of other spiritual seekers, or renounce who they were and go into a monastic institute. With the advent of modern churches, the internet, and podcasts, one does not have to go wandering anymore, yet this does not stop people from doing just that. Millions of pilgrims walk the earth in search of some form of spiritual experience. Each of us can become a pilgrim in our own everyday life. Spiritual wandering can be as simple as a morning walk in the park and being fully present and aware of everything that surrounds you.

Have you ever walked in the park and practiced the "I am that, I am" exercise? I heard about this process on a tele-seminar with Neil Donald Walsch, in which he talked about finding God and the self in the world around us. In this exercise, as you walk, look to a tree and say, "I am that, I am." Then you see a flower and say, "I am that, I am." You may see a fellow parkgoer and say, "I am that, I am." This inner dialogue becomes a mantra inside your head, a point of focus that grounds you totally in the moment with no separation between you and the world outside of you. This is a fabulous wandering Hierophant exercise, and you don't even have to do it at a park. You can do it anywhere—the mall, hiking through the mountains, walking along the beach. The point is not the location, but the dropping of the ego "I" and the embrace of the "I" that is nothing and everything, much the way millions of spiritual seekers before you have sought to find who they are by forgetting who they used to be.

6. THE LOVERS

I always find it interesting that most people presume that the Lovers card is about bringing someone else into their lives, and that this card symbolizes a certain stage of maturation that dictates a time of matchup or joining with another to carry on to the next phases of life. I will admit this is one way of looking at the Lovers, but I do find it a very limiting and narrow way to view this card. For me, the story of this card lies more in its number allocation than in its title. The number six is focused more on the idea of relationships and commitments, sometimes with other people, but mostly with ourselves. In many respects, this card tests our resolve to walk a certain path, to be and act a certain way, and to think about who and what we interact with as we continue on the journey we started back at the Fool card. The Lovers asks us who and what we are committed to. This question needs to be answered honestly.

The longest relationship we have is with ourselves. It is the one relationship we should be constantly fostering, nurturing, and deepening. So how is your relationship with you? Are you on good terms with yourself, or are you committed to beating yourself up and setting yourself up for failure? Repeating destructive patterns of behavior generally lets us know we are committed to making life difficult for ourselves, and in turn difficult for those around us. Choosing to be committed to a joyful, loving, and peaceful path generally means your life flows pretty well, and you find yourself supported by loving, joyful, peaceful people in return. Your life is a commitment, but what you have committed to will be showcased here in the Lovers card. Good or bad is irrelevant, as you can choose to change your journey, change your commitments, and deepen your relationship with the one person who matters the most: you.

Intentional

For this exercise, you are going to write up a self-care regimen and make a commitment to follow through with it. Self-care is an expression of self-love. When we learn to put ourselves first, we are acknowledging that we matter and that we see ourselves as important. If our relationship with our self is solid, committed, and filled with love, then so too are all of our other relationships. In essence, this is using the Lovers card in the most intentional and deliberate way.

Most times people will say they have a wonderful self-care regimen in place, so I ask them to describe it. This is where things tend to unravel, mainly because most of us don't really make a firm commitment to self-care. Most of us, myself included, tend to see self-care as a luxury; it's something that there isn't always time, money, or space for. The truth is, self-care is the one thing we should be making our number one priority. Self-care doesn't have to be all bubble baths and massages, but if that is yours, fabulous! Self-care is also having quiet time alone, when you won't be distracted or interrupted. It can be taking yourself out for a morning walk and letting your body and mind relax. It can be a yoga class, a daily salad, a ten-minute meditation, or a mani-pedi. It really doesn't matter what you do, just how consistent you are in doing it. This is the commitment part, the follow through, the point of accountability, the real intentional lesson of the path of the Lovers. Commit, show up, follow-through.

Intuitive

For something totally different, turn your Lovers card upside down and purposely put this card and the energy that surrounds it in a protective bubble. Close your eyes and allow yourself to go back in time to immerse yourself in a period when you first met your spouse or significant other, when you first realized you were part of a family, or that very first moment you decided you were going to be best friends with someone. Really put yourself back into the shoes of your former self. While you are there, take note of what type of person you were at this time. Who was the person who formed all of these relationships that your present self has to live with?

Sometimes when I do this exercise with my private clients they don't even recognize the people they see back at the moment of their relationship conceptions, which, to be honest, is to be expected as we all grow, change, and evolve. But the real question is, have your relationships done the same, or are you still trying to have the same relationship you had back when you were all different people? Use all of this information as a point of meditation. Allow yourself to really go deep with this exercise, especially if one of your current relationships is having problems or seems off track. You may find plenty to journal about later, but for now just meditate. Go back and follow the threads. See what has gone well and what perhaps may need some healing, love, and possible mending. Stay in reflection until you feel you cannot focus anymore, then grab your journal and dump your findings onto its pages.

Wandering

For this exercise, pick one thing you are currently working on manifesting. It might be a new job, a new creative project, a new house, or even a new lover. Hold it in your mind's eye and then fast-forward to the moment after you have manifested your heart's desire—where your future self is basking in the glow of the Lovers energy coming together. Now, let that future self take your current self for a walk backward in time. Your future self, the self that is already living the life you are only currently dreaming about, is going to show you what happened to make your dream into a reality. Do not try to control this journey, just let it unfold in your mind's eye like a movie.

Right now you are purely an observer, collecting information that you will use to shore up your commitment to seeing this goal or dream through. When you are working tirelessly on a dream or goal and aren't really seeing big changes around you, it is easy to become despondent, to stop your self-care, and to question your choices. By using this process with the Lovers card you are reconnecting your heart energy back to your goal or dream, as well as reenergizing your commitment to it. When we start from the end and remind ourselves just how amazing life is going to be when we pull this dream or goal off, we get a new burst of energy and a new sense of purpose. So go on, let your future self be your guide and go take a walk on the manifestation side of the street.

7. THE CHARIOT

If we are to view the Chariot in the order it lands in the major arcana, we could say that this card represents the idea of moving out of your parents' house and heading off into the world to start your own family or your own adventure. The Chariot card comes after the Lovers card, which can sometimes, but not always, show a coupling. Only a few cards before it we were learning from mother (Empress), father (Emperor), Auntie (the High Priestess), and Uncle (the

Hierophant). If we view the first seven cards of the major arcana as what happens to us as we grow inside a family unit, when the Chariot rolls up, we know it's time to pack our things and leave the security of the family home behind to head off into the world and make our mark. Given the time when the tarot was created, around the middle of the fifteenth century, this is exactly how life would have been, not to mention this point in our lives would have happened sooner rather than later, probably around fourteen to sixteen years of age. It is hard to imagine in today's world being sent off at such an early age to start a family and provide for yourself financially. Leaving home is our first taste of life-altering change. We are literally moved out of our comfort zone and placed in situations that have tremendously sharp learning curves. Some take to these new conditions quickly and easily while others struggle and stumble.

Can you remember what it was like when you left home, how that movement changed all the aspects of your life? How did you manage it? Was it something you flowed with or something you really struggled with? The need for upheaval, the need to change and move away from where you are, is not something everyone jumps for joy about. Leaving one's comfort zone can create fear in some, and fear makes for a terrible navigator. It is hard to think about the road you need to travel and the best route to get you from where you are to where you need to be when fear is yelling in your ear. Just know the Chariot doesn't really care how you get to where you are going, and it doesn't even really care what condition you are in when you arrive at your destination. All it knows is that you are going, whether you like it or not.

PATHWORK

Intentional

What areas of your life do you need to move on from, or, alternatively, what areas of your life do you need to drive toward? Trying to stay tethered to something while driving in the opposite direction is a fabulous way of totaling your Chariot, so stop, take a breath, close your eyes, and concentrate. What direction do you really need to be heading and how long is it going to take you to reach your destination? Now consider what you will need to leave behind, what you need to untether from so you can have forward movement. We don't often think of loss when we see the Chariot card, but loss and gain go hand in hand. Moving is not always easy, nor is the road paved with guarantees, but sometimes we have no choice, and oftentimes the move is worth it in the long run. Use the answers to the questions in this exercise as points of meditation and dig deep to find out what really lies behind all of those fears and doubts that keep you tied to the very thing you are trying to drive your Chariot away from. Keep in mind that this won't be the last change you see in the major arcana, as this movement here is only the first of many to come, so it is better to find those pesky excuses now and start weeding them out.

Intuitive

The Chariot is associated with the watery sign of Cancer. Those born in the sign of Cancer can be restless, always looking to the next adventure, even though they do tend to be homebodies. Travel, in many respects, keeps a Cancer's water flowing. Go and pull your Chariot card from your deck and place it picture side up somewhere you can see it. Then gather some magazines, scissors, paste, and a sheet of cardboard (recommendation: 8.5 x 5.5 inches). For this exercise, you are going to use your Chariot to help you create a mini vision board for your dream vacation. Before you begin ripping, cutting, and pasting your pictures onto your cardboard, close your eyes just for a minute and conjure the vision of yourself having this amazing vacation. Hold the vision for as long as you can, then start on your mini vision board. This exercise is just as good as going on the vacation, as far as your energy is concerned. This very hands-on act will let the Chariot work through you, moving blocks and getting all four of your wheels firmly back on the path of your life. Once you have finished your vision board you can put it next to your Chariot card and light a candle, saying a simple prayer of gratitude for the journey, the adventure, and the trip of a lifetime, ramping up the manifestation energy both the Chariot card and your mini vision board provide.

Wandering

Let's just say for a minute that you have crashed your Chariot. The wheels have fallen off and there is no way it can possibly be driven. You have one choice: leave it where it is and start walking. As your feet hit the path, which way are they headed? Knowing which way you're headed is important, as each direction comes with its own meaning. So stop for a moment and notice which way your feet are instinctually pointed, as this direction has a message for you. North is the direction of inspiration and enlightened expression. South is the direction of passion, driven adventure, and movement. East is the direction of new opportunities and beginnings. And west is the direction of past issues and things coming to an end. Sometimes the most powerful lessons are the ones that are created out of things gone horribly wrong. So look at your feet, see where they are pointed, and move toward this new direction in your life.

8. STRENGTH

This card could very well be called courage, for strength and courage seem to be only separated by the slightest of degrees. Just like courage, Strength comes in varied forms and means different things, depending on the context in which it is being used. Strength could be physical, emotional, intellectual, or spiritual. It could also be compassion and kindness, which are other elements of courage. We all require different facets of strength, depending on the challenges we face, what problems we wish to solve, or what new and scary dream we wish to pursue; and of course, where there is strength, courage, and compassion, there will be fear, doubt, and anger. It is as if one cannot get to Strength without first having to walk through one of its opposing gatekeepers. They are, for the most part, mutual allies, even though it may not seem that way initially. Often we don't even know how strong, courageous, or compassionate we are until we come face-to-face with our darkest fears or our most dreaded circumstances. Perhaps this is why the Strength card comes right after the Chariot, and after we experience our first real life change within the journey of the major arcana.

There are many obstacles and challenges that your current journey will bring. Some will terrify you and others will reveal parts of yourself that you never knew existed. The Strength card lets you know that in many ways, your current set of circumstances is shaping you as a person. It is molding you into the person you will become, so it might be a good idea to see if this process is forming a future for you that is aligned with your dreams and goals, or if you are just recreating the same person you have always been. This is what walking with the Strength card is all about. It is a slow and gradual transformation and one that will change who you are forever. Once you move on from this card there will be no going back to the person you used to be. Instead you will forge on ahead as the person this card shaped you to be.

PATHWORK

Intentional

Go ahead and pull the Strength card from your deck and lay it down faceup in front of you. Keep the remainder of the deck in your hands and shuffle it gently as you ask the Strength card a question. Your question is this: How might I best use you today? Once you have asked your question and feel you have shuffled your cards enough, hold the deck close to your chest in between your closed palms, fingers pointed up. Take three nice deep breaths and then open your hands and split your deck. The card that is on top and facing you is the answer to your question. Place it down next to the Strength card. These two cards will be your guiding energy today. Keep them somewhere you can see them as you move about your day; maybe even take a picture of them and make them the lock screen of your phone if you have to work or travel and can't take your tarot cards with you. Each time you see these two cards, remember that the card that answered your question is the path to service today.

Intuitive

The Strength card in the Animal Totem Tarot was created to show what happens when strength is seen as a burden. The ox is strong, but his strength is used not for himself but in servitude to others. This idea that strength itself is not something favorable may seem to go against the grain of how most people think, as we often believe that courage, fortitude, and might are positive traits. But how many times have your gifts been a burden? This burden is exactly what we are going to meditate on today. Take some nice deep breaths and bring to mind the last time someone asked you to use your gift or your strength in a way that felt heavy or uncomfortable to you. Bring it to your mind's eye and see it in full color. Take another nice deep breath and simply observe the feelings that come up as you watch the scene over again in your mind. Don't make any judgments, just let the movie play along. Take another nice deep breath and now repeat this mantra: "My gift is not a burden and I am sorry for making it feel unloved. I love it and I am grateful I have it in my life." Again, do not force anything; just keep breathing and reciting your mantra. If it feels more comfortable to close your eyes, please do so. Continue with this meditation and mantra until you feel complete. Take another nice deep breath and ground your energy back into your body and the room you find yourself in. If you want to explore this deeper, pick up your journal and write your findings in it. If not, just know you shifted a lot of energy in that small meditation, and it will make you stronger and more confident moving forward.

Wandering

How often do you think about this card in reverse or upside down? There is something very liberating about starting your quest for strength backward. In other words, take time to lean into all of the excuses, all of the fears, and all of the doubts that stop you from doing things you claim you want to do. Humans are highly creative beings, and the number of excuses we make or reasons we give on a daily basis is quite staggering. Today, stop and pay attention every time you hear yourself saying "I can't," for at the core of all these "I can't" statements are two very powerful emotions: fear and doubt. These two emotions tell a story. Every time you find yourself saying no to something, it is your upside down Strength card story playing out. Each time you listen to your story, ask yourself if what you are listening to is based on fact and if you have any real evidence that the story has merit. This exercise is not so much about facing your fears, or even overcoming them, but more about seeing them for what they are: a story you have created to stop you from moving out of your current situation.

9. THE HERMIT

Guide, teacher, and keeper of the path, the Hermit can represent the need to go on a spirit or vision quest. I am not speaking of the type where you take mind-altering drugs, but rather a period of deep meditation, inner reflection, and a shadow walk along all the small paths that have led you to this place, or this moment. The Hermit knows how this work is to be conducted and he also knows the places in the mind you will need to go. This is why he holds the lamp and acts as your guide. He knows where to take you, when to leave you to your own thoughts, and when to come back and get you. It is comforting to know that you will not be forgotten or abandoned on your quest, and to know that someone else will be holding space and watching over you as you do your cleaning and clearing work. In this respect, the Hermit may represent one of your personal healing guides, like an angel or ascended master, or even a totem animal. It doesn't matter how you see the Hermit or what he or she shape-shifts into, just as long as you have the Hermit with you as you embark on your journey. The best quests have a specific intention, specified start and finish points, and a desired result in mind. Although you don't have to share this information with the Hermit, it may be beneficial for you to do so. Let's start with the most important question of all: What is it you seek? Clear the chatter and distractions from your mind and allow space for the question to present itself. Just know this: once your quest has begun, the only way out is to complete it. You can take as much time as you want, for physical time has no meaning in the Hermit's world, and even when you think you are rushing, you are probably still taking more time than you could possibly imagine.

PATHWORK

Intentional

There comes a time when we all need a little quiet. A time when we can get the noise of the world out of our heads and empty our minds. This is what the Hermit is good at: providing space—quiet, still, sacred space. Go ahead and pull the Hermit card out of your deck and place it somewhere you can see it. Now grab your calendar, datebook, or planner. For this exercise you are going to deliberately create space for yourself in your schedule. Even if it is only ten minutes a day. This is a time when you will be in Hermit mode. Keep your Hermit card in your line of vision as you create space over the next week. Find gaps or shift things around so you are giving yourself time for nothing at all. Make sure you black it out in your datebook, calendar, or planner so you don't fill up the time with something else. This is an exercise I make my clients do on a regular basis. Creating space has become hard for people to do. They are more apt to fill it rather than just allow it to be empty. Once you have blacked out your Hermit time, light a candle and offer up a prayer or mantra of thanks to the Hermit card.

Intuitive

The Hermit doesn't just offer us space to clear our heads; this card also offers light to shine into the dark corners of our lives that we may not otherwise be able to see. The Hermit's lamp is the lamp of truth; it shines light where there is a need for healing and clearing. To help you find what those areas of your life are, follow this simple three-card spread. Grab a deck of cards and remove the Hermit card. Place it faceup in front of you and focus on it as you begin to slowly shuffle your cards. As you shuffle, ask the Hermit the following question: What areas of my current life need to be healed, forgiven, and let go of?

Once you feel you have shuffled enough, place your deck close to your heart and ask your question two more times. Now go ahead and pull your three cards and place them in a line under your Hermit card. Card one is what needs to be healed, card two is what needs to be forgiven, and card three is what needs to be cut loose. Just take a moment with your spread before you try to read it. Take a couple of nice deep breaths and ground yourself before you reach for your journal or tarot notebook to dive deeper into the three cards that now lie before you. Once you feel your reading is complete, thank the Hermit for sharing the wisdom of his lamp's light and put your cards away.

Wandering

During the Middle Ages it was very common for holy mystics, ascetics, and monastics to wander from town to town taking alms and providing spiritual enlightenment. These holy men and women had no possessions and lived a nomadic life. The Hermit reminds me of these early spiritual teachers. Their concern was to be in the world, but not to be a part of it, and to acknowledge they were having a physical experience but were experiencing a spiritual journey. There was a distinct separation from their life choices and the rest of society, and in this respect they were what today we would call "fringe dwellers." This is also where the Hermit resides: on the fringe, the outskirts, separate but part of. As you make your way through your day, see if you can keep some distance between you and the rest of the world as you observe and don't interfere. Find places where you can only speak when someone asks something of you and take note if slipping into the shadows is easy or difficult for you, as these will be things for you to meditate on at a later date. Happy wandering, you spiritual mystic you.

10. THE WHEEL OF FORTUNE

Every time I come before the wheel I see something different. Each time it turns it presents a new opportunity for knowledge and understanding of what it means to be having a human experience as a spiritual being. Sometimes the wheel reminds me of the cycle of birth, living, and death. Other times it reminds me of the never-ending loop of what the Buddhists call *samsara*, the cyclic loop of suffering. And other times it reminds me that nothing is permanent. What is "now" won't be later on; seasons change and with them so do the conditions in which you live. No matter what lesson the wheel brings with it, there is always one common element, and that is cyclic change. For me, this is the fortune element of the card: that things change, that life is fluid, and that nothing ever stays the same. If you have ever experienced dark moments in your life, then you too would have to rejoice in the fact that change is inevitable. How horrid would it be to know that if you hit a bad patch in your life, you'd be stuck with it until death? For this I always give thanks to the wheel. It is time to decide how you will move forward within the cycle of your existence. Will you continue your spiritual work and seek to rid yourself of the Samsara experience? Perhaps you will look at your life as many acts and decide which goals you would like to achieve within those acts, or maybe you will totally freak out and find yourself rooted to the spot in the knowledge that the experience you are having now won't last forever. Attachment to moments of time and to fleeting feelings usually occurs when things are going blissfuly right in our lives. And although there is nothing wrong with seeking joy at every turn, to do so in the hopes of avoiding pain and suffering will only allow you to experience joy in a limited and fearful way. The wheel says embrace it all, for the change is the constant, and within it you will always have what you need and your soul will be fulfilled.

PATHWORK

Intentional

For this exercise, we are going to look at money blocks, because luck won't do you much good if you are blocked and can't see it when it shows up. The Wheel of Fortune is one of those cards that a lot of people associate with money, which is interesting considering its humble origins. In modern tarot, money, luck, and success seem to play a larger part than they did back in the fifteenth century. In this respect, the Wheel of Fortune can be used for those wanting to deal with money blocks or increase their luck, though you really will need to be specific, otherwise your Wheel of Fortune will turn into a roulette wheel and your bets may sink you. So go ahead and remove your Wheel of Fortune card from your deck and place it faceup in front of you. Leave some space, as you are going to add four other cards around it. Pick up the remainder of your deck and give it a shuffle. When you are done, take the card from the top of your deck and place it above your Wheel of Fortune card; this card represents your current money blessings. Take the next card from your deck and place it below your Wheel of Fortune card; this card represents your current money block. Take the next card from the top of your deck and place it to the right of your Wheel of Fortune card; this card shows how your money blocks are interfering with your luck. Now take the last card from the bottom of your deck and place it to the left of the Wheel of Fortune card; this card shows you the key to removing your block and getting your Wheel turning again. You should have a total of five cards faceup in front of you, with the Wheel of Fortune in the middle, surrounded by four other cards. Take your time with these cards and work your way slowly around the Wheel. Grab your journal and take notes if you feel inclined.

Intuitive

The Wheel of Fortune is a fabulous card to journey with during the changing of the seasons. I often sit with this card in meditation during the Winter and Summer Solstices as well as the Spring and Fall Equinoxes. Each season brings with it change, a new gift, a new blessing, and a new way to let go. The seasons mean different things to each of us, and we all have our favorites. My favorite season is autumn, and it is also my most abundant season. Because of this, I am constantly on the lookout for abundant opportunities that will be ready for harvest come autumn. Your season could be totally different. For this exercise, you will spend time meditating on your favorite season. You will contemplate why you enjoy this season and what sort of feelings it fills you with every time the Wheel turns and brings it into your experience. Truly immerse yourself in your season. Feel the air on your skin, smell the scents this season brings, and focus on the sounds and noises associated with this particular season. Be one with it, and allow it to show you the gifts and blessings it offers. You can do this immersion exercise anytime you want and as often as you want, as there is no reason not to connect with the energy of your season whenever and wherever you feel necessary.

Wandering

The Wheel of Fortune spins and turns, and it never stays in the same place for long. It is a teacher of temporary existence and the normality of constant change. The question is, do you know where on the Wheel you are? Knowing where you are gives you an idea of where you might be headed, or what sort of change you may be able to face. In some ways, we walk the complete Wheel in a twenty-four-hour cycle. We begin at one point in the morning and wander around the Wheel during the day until we find ourselves back where we started in the evening. For me, my beginning and ending points would be in bed. I start the day there, and that is also where I end the day. You, however, might consider the starting points and ending points of your Wheel in other ways. Knowing where your Wheel starts and ends gives you a clearer idea of where you are on the Wheel. If we use the Wheel of Fortune to map our goals and dreams then you would also have very clear beginning and ending points, which would again make it somewhat easier to find out where you are. Your task for this exercise is to first establish where you want to focus the energy of your Wheel. Is it on your life, your day, your year, or your current project? Next, walk your Wheel and find out where you are. Then take a few steps ahead of where you now stand and peek down the path to see if you can predict what is coming, what you need to change in order to make what's coming easier to deal with, and who you need to be when what is coming shows up. By walking around your personal Wheel of Fortune you will learn about how abundance energy is created, circulated, and changed. This will get you into the flow of the Wheel's movement rather than constantly feeling like it is running you over on its way to somewhere else. Walking the Wheel may not feel natural or normal initially, but stick with it and it will end up being an invaluable skill.

11. JUSTICE

Are you someone who can naturally see both sides of a situation, or is your side the only side that gets your attention? Justice seeks to know all factors and all perspectives before she is willing to cast forth a ruling. Perhaps this is because of Justice's connection to Venus and the Empress. Just like these two goddesses, she wants all of those in her charge to feel heard, validated, and relevant. This is not always easy, and sometimes she has to use varying methods to make sure all who come before her get the justice that is divinely and rightfully theirs. Justice knows her decisions have rippling consequences, many of which will send out aftershocks long after her ruling has been read. Knowing what has been, what is, and what will be are all things that this card has to reconcile. You might think this sounds somewhat like the hand of karma, and maybe in some cases that is the role that Justice plays, but other times she is merely assisting you to stay on your soul path, regardless of what that path is. It is not her place to cast a judgement on the journey of your soul; it is only her place to judge how you choose to walk that path in regard to your engagement with others who walk alongside you. This is where elements of Justice can be perceived as unfair, as you might feel that others seem to be rewarded for bad behavior, whereas those you love seem to be punished for being decent, rule-following people. Sometimes it can be hard to see how Justice can justify her decisions. It is not easy to trust in the larger picture and the part we play in it, for oftentimes we don't know what that is or how we are even engaging in it. Sometimes you have to trust that what seems unfair in the current moment will end up being one of the best things to happen in the long term.

PATHWORK

Intentional

Justice understands only too well that what one puts out in the world is what one gets back from the world. This is where the focus or your meditation needs to be. Remove your Justice card from your deck and place it either on your altar or somewhere it will be safe and you can light a candle next to it, as you are going to use the flickering flame as a point of focus. Next, get comfortable and take a few nice deep breaths, in through the nose and out through the mouth. Just allow yourself to settle and stay focused on the flame. As you keep your eyes on the flame, send it the gratitude, love, and appreciation you have for your life. Size is not important in this exercise, so even if it is something small that you are grateful for, send it to the flame. Keep sending this energy to your flame until you feel you have nothing left to send. Watch the flame as it reacts to all you have mentally sent its way. Take a few nice deep breaths and end your meditation. Gather your Justice card and your journal and write down anything that you observed about the flame. You can go ahead and blow the candle out if you wish. It does not need to keep burning now that you are done. This quick, simple meditation helps you focus on sending positive energy into the world around you. Practice it as often as you like.

Intuitive

The scales of Justice are almost mythical things. Take the scales of Ma'at of ancient Egypt for example; it is said she used her scales to weigh a person's heart after their death to see if it was as light as a feather. If it was, they were allowed to pass on to a happier, more peaceful realm in the afterlife. If not, well, I think you get the idea. This meant that if one had lived a loving, caring, compassionate life, their heart would not be weighed down with fear, anger, hate, or regret after death. We often forget about the things that weigh us down, or more to the point, things that weigh our hearts down. Sadness, blame, shame, and guilt would not leave one's heart light as a feather, nor would living an angry, bitter existence filled with regret and contempt.

Using the scales from the Justice card, can you find the places in your own heart that are heavy? Settle yourself and calm your breathing. Call on Ma'at and ask her for guidance on how to lighten your heart and release the load you carry around inside your chest. Use the scales as a focal point for your meditation—watch them dip, fall, or balance with each thought or feeling you have. Do not judge; just observe and write about your findings later in your journal, if you wish to pick them apart for further analysis.

Wandering

Would you want to spend a day in the Justice's shoes? Most people think it would be easy or fun to dish out justice to those they feel have wronged them or the world in some way, but the truth is not everything is as it seems, and what you think you know may not be the truth Justice herself seeks. Righting wrongs is not what Justice does, but instead she must find balance, order, and true resolution, not just in this world, but in all of the worlds that have been and gone, and all that are yet to come. Just for today, I want you to imagine yourself in Justice's seat. I want you to feel the weight of the scales in your hand, and I want you to understand that you are solely responsible for keeping them balanced. Under no circumstances can the scales tip too much in one direction. You must do your best to move throughout your whole day keeping them as balanced as possible. The longer you carry around the scales, the more you are going to understand how complex Justice's job really is, for you will soon discover that it is not easy to keep the peace. It is not simple to keep the scales where they need to be, and it is far too easy to weigh down one side, and stop thinking about the other side while you do. This exercise will not only deepen your appreciation for this card, but it will also expand your awareness to how Justice plays out in you, your life, and the larger world of your experiences and relationships.

12. THE HANGED MAN

The Hanged Man is probably one of my most loved cards for meditation. Letting go, surrendering, and putting one's heart above one's head are lessons we all struggle with. Yet the Hanged Man does these things deliberately and intentionally. He puts himself into this position on purpose, so that he can focus on releasing his ego's control. It never ceases to amaze me just how many people see the act of surrender as something passive or submissive, like these two things show some sort of flaw or weakness in the individual willingly giving up their need to be in control. I have seen this play out time and time again with people convinced that their life is on the wrong path and that they need to spend as much time, money, and energy as possible to find the path they should be on, never wanting to surrender to the fact that our soul path is the only path we walk, and this path was selected by each of us many lifetimes before. The more one looks outside of oneself for a purpose or reason to be, the more lost one becomes. The Hanged Man knows this, which is why he ties himself to a tree, or in the case of the Animal Totem Tarot, surrenders himself to be of divine service to others. Can you imagine giving up your hopes and dreams to benefit others? Can you even contemplate living a life in total submission? The Hanged Man's lessons are hard—there is just no way around that—but they are important, for it is at the point of surrender that one truly becomes powerful. It is only when we let go of desire that we can have anything we want. It is only when we release the ego mind that the soul can finally show us the miracles of the divine path we were born to walk. Your power to create only magnifies when you no longer want anything. Irony is a big player in the energy of this card.

So are you ready to let it all go? Can you give up your struggle for just a little while and see what possibilities the Hanged Man has to offer? Choose carefully as you make your way through the pathwork exercises below.

PATHWORK

Intentional

The Hanged Man has deliberately and intentionally chosen to see the world differently, to shift his perspective and look at things from another angle. This card is a constant reminder that we tend to fall into habitual ways of seeing, which in turn make us act in a preprogrammed way. I know we all like to think we have free will and make decisions based on awareness, but unless we are truly coming at something outside of our normal way of dealing with situations, people, or problems, we are actually running on a habitual loop. The Hanged

Man challenges this instinctive habit by turning himself upside down. He literally puts his head down and takes a look around at his world from a different position. For the next few days, see if you can do the same. Every time you do a reading, spread, or daily one-card draw, turn your cards upside down. Change the way they present themselves and suddenly your message is coming from a totally different place. The best way to start seeing things from the Hanged Man's viewpoint is to look at the colors, the shapes, and the things you never noticed before when you or your cards were right side up. How differently does your eye move over the images now that they are not the way you are used to seeing them? Think about how this card could be used as a mirror of what is currently going on in your life or how the cards might be protecting you. To explore the mirror or protection aspects of your upside down cards, consider using my book *Tarot Reversals for Beginners*. The Hanged Man says that wisdom comes to those who choose to view the world from an uncomfortable position. Hanging upside down by one foot sure seems uncomfortable to me!

Intuitive

The Hanged Man is associated with the watery and intuitive energy of Neptune, which connects this card to the zodiac sign of Pisces, which in turn links us to the Knight of Cups. That is the trifecta of vision quests right there, which makes the Hanged Man the ideal card to use when you want to dive deeper with your dreamwork. For this exercise, try sleeping with the Hanged Man under your pillow, or even just place the card where you can see it as you drift off to sleep and as you wake up. As you settle into bed for the night, ask the Hanged Man the following question: What area of my life do I need to surrender control over?

Just pose the question to the card and set the intention that the answer will be given to you while you sleep. As you wake up in the morning and gaze at the card, say, "Remind me throughout the day where I need to let go and trust." Notice if this small exercise changes how you dream or how your day unfolds.

Wandering

If you truly want to get into the upside-down shoes of the Hanged Man, do yoga. The best way to pathwork with the Hanged Man is through yoga. It is not only meditative, as each pose is designed to get you out of your ever-chattering mind and into a state of shifted perception, but it also engages the body-mind dynamic that we are seriously trying to cultivate here in the wandering section of this book. I have had some of my most amazing meditative moments while in the middle of a yoga class. I have been able to still my mind, drop the "I" and drift off toward the void. The best part about yoga is that there are classes for everyone. Acro-yoga, hot yoga, and lots of other types in between. I myself like kundalini yoga. The point of yoga is to get you out of your habitual mind and to expand your sense of awareness. Some of the poses I have done over the years just don't make any logical sense, which is the point. Putting oneself upside down to hang by one leg doesn't make logical sense either, but here the Hanged Man is. So go wander with the Hanged Man, find a yoga that will work for you, strike a pose, and let the release of the logical, habitual mind begin.

13. DEATH

It is no mistake that Death follows the Hanged Man, and that after a time of enforced surrender and an extended period of not moving, we step into the realm of death. This is the death of the ego-self, the one that we let go of while hanging upside down. It is a spiritual death, one through which the past self, the self that no longer serves our current state of being and is no longer relevant, ceases to exist once and for all. Shedding this skin and letting go of this part of who we used to be lays the groundwork for rebirth, regeneration, and a new form to experience and engage in the world around us. Learning how to let go of our need to control, learning how to stop pushing and forcing things into existence, and learning how to go with the flow are skills only the Hanged Man of the previous card can teach. It is through this surrender that we learn to die, release our attachments, and find our way back into the loving arms of the spiritual side of who we are. When we are not afraid of dying, we can move toward Death with open arms. We can embrace this opportunity to be born again and allow ourselves to slip into a new skin. That is really all any of this is, a constant cycle of rebirth, with Death as the recycling agent. Death also lets us know that something has come to an end in order for something new to begin. Endings have to happen in order for beginnings to occur. Trees must blossom before they bear fruit. The blossom must die and fall away to make place for the fruit to burst forth. Considering the journey you have taken so far through the major arcana, Death was bound to happen, for there is no way you could be the same person now as you were when you began this journey. There are parts of you that just no longer exist. These parts could be thoughts, beliefs, emotions, goals, or dreams. What you wished for or wanted and desired at the beginning of this journey may no longer seem relevant or important anymore. This shows the evolving being that you are, with fluid thoughts, feelings, and beliefs. This new level of awareness moved you out of the ego mind, and now you will have to find a new way to chart your course.

PATHWORK

Intentional

The Death card has fascinating numbers. Thirteen in numerology is a karmic debt number and is linked to the need to burn off karma through the act of hard work, which sure gives the phrase "working yourself to death" a new twist. Thirteen is also a four, once we break it down by each digit (1 + 3 = 4), which connects it to the Emperor, who ironically is a true workaholic. Four is a foundation number, as it is the number that makes it possible for everything else to be built. From this perspective, the Death card shows us that in many ways our work is never done, that we are always building and re-building, and that we are always in the throes of one karmic cycle after another. This is the cycle of life—constant and ever moving, transforming and refiguring itself. This will be your point of focus for this exercise, the idea of surrendering to your karmic debt. But how do you know what it is? Take Death out of your deck and place it faceup in front of you, then shuffle the remaining cards until you feel you are done. Hold the cards up to your heart and take a few nice, deep, grounding breaths. When you feel settled, say the following to your cards: "Show me my current karmic debt and how to burn it off."

Then split your deck, creating two piles. Take the top card of the left pile and the bottom card of the right pile and lay them faceup under your Death card. The top card you pulled from the left pile is what needs to be burned off and given back to Death; the bottom card from your right pile is how Death feels it needs to be done. You may wish to pick up your journal and explore these two cards further. Especially the numbers on each of the cards, as these may also be clues that can help move you forward.

Intuitive

Although technically we don't look at this card from a literal death perspective, there is an element of it attached to this card. Like it or not, our lives will end. We will cease to exist and perhaps even be forgotten. These are not comfortable thoughts and feelings to deal with. The idea that our time here is pointless, inconsequential, and lacking meaning makes us all shift a little in our seats. We like to think we have a purpose and a reason for being. Many spiritual teachers argue that this attachment, this holding on to a temporary life, stops us from truly loving and engaging with the flickering moments we do have, and that this level of false living only brings us great suffering. This is the level of reflection the Death card presents. It asks you to sit with this idea of attachment and suffering to see if you can find truth of it in your life, and to meditate on the idea that all things are temporary, including yourself. It also asks you to ponder the importance of the things you have gathered in your life and to question your need to hang on to them so tightly. As you meditate on these questions, see where you can find points of liberation, moments of peace, and an easing of stress. You will be amazed at how all of that "holding on" energy has been affecting your body.

Wandering

What's coming to an end in your life? There is no escaping the fact that death is all around us. With everything we do and everywhere we go, death is there. It has to be, or we would never see birth. But understanding that birth and death are the same energy takes a certain amount of awareness, which is why it is good to deliberately walk around seeking this energy, looking for its magic, and exploring its miracles. Where there was once a dead spot in an urban area now there may be a thriving community garden. Where there was once a war zone, now there is a flourishing village. Where there was once an environmental nightmare, now there is a nature reserve and protected site. For this exercise, seek out places in your community that have been repurposed, that have been resurrected and brought with them the miracle of new life. If you can't find any in your local area, find an example of one online and use it as a point of mental wandering about the miracle of death and rebirth. By seeing how life follows death, you learn to let things go with more ease. Go now and walk Death's path and feel Death's energy, as it takes one thing so another can be blessed in its remains. Get comfortable in Death's shoes so you can see the miracle that is life.

14. TEMPERANCE

Temperance sits between Death and the Devil. She bridges who you were with the possibilities of who you could be. She stands ready to heal your wounds and prepare you for what lies beyond in the Devil's playground. In this respect, Temperance takes past, present, and future and molds them together to create something completely new. You are not who you once were, and now she needs to mold your new image. This requires balance, expertise, and refinement, since she must attend to the afterbirth of your new self while cleaning up the mess left behind from the death of the ego. She does all of this while preparing you to walk through the residual energy of your past self. This residual energy will be in abundance once you cross over to the Devil card. Temperance's work is complicated, specialized, and unique, as she must change and alter her healing techniques for every individual that crosses her path. What works for you will not work for the next person who comes to her healing waters. Temperance is a magician in her own right, molding and weaving together elements to make something beautiful, resilient, and strong. She takes her task very seriously, and when you stand before her, you will have all of her attention. Having someone this focused on you and your well-being may be new to you, and it could make you feel uncomfortable and exposed. In your very raw state, this level of exposure may make you feel anxious and even slightly paranoid. Temperance is going to see things that you and other people may have missed, such as details and information that will help you navigate your next steps. Therefore, ask her questions, ask her what she sees, ask her for guidance and for words of advice. Ask as many questions as you can think of, because once you leave Temperance behind, her healing magic and her focus will shift to the next person.

PATHWORK

Intentional

Temperance is best known for bringing two opposing elements together and making something beautiful and unique with them. This is why she is often referred to as the alchemist. She can basically take something that others would discard or look over and make it something precious and desirable.

Remove the Temperance card from your deck and place it faceup in front of you. Shuffle the remaining cards and ask Temperance what two elements or things she wants you to blend together. Shuffle the cards until you feel ready, then fan them out in front of you. Scan your hand over the cards and select the two cards that either heat up or give off a prickling feeling in your palm. Turn your two cards over and have a look to see what trick Temperance wants you to pull off. You may wish to journal with these cards for a while, as making a recipe for these two cards might take you some time. Just trust that the two cards you have drawn are the correct ones. Do not be tempted to put them back in the deck and try again just because you don't like the pair you have been given. Remember, Temperance sees things others miss. She knows what ingredients you need. All you have to do is blend them.

Intuitive

Temperance has a long connection to the rainbow. Even in my very own Animal Totem Tarot, we see a flamingo that has a rainbow being formed by the waterfall behind it. In the original Rider-Waite-Smith image, the artist was very heavily influenced by the goddess Iris, who was the personification of the rainbow and was said to be a messenger from God. In today's spiritual community, you often hear how loved ones have crossed over the rainbow bridge, meaning they have passed away, which is interesting, as Temperance is considered a bridge. Mix Iris and Temperance together, and you have a rainbow bridge crossing from the heavens to the earth plane and back again. This is a wonderful image to meditate on, to see the rainbow as a sort of heavenly conveyor belt. Get yourself comfortable and take a few nice deep breaths. Visualize the answers and solutions to your problems and questions sliding down the rainbow into Temperance's arms, as she mixes you a drink while you pull up a seat at her spiritual bar. Just picture yourself sipping on something cool and smooth as all of the things you ever wanted come gliding down the rainbow bridge. Know that each sip of the cocktail Temperance has mixed for you is healing your body, calming your mind, and restoring your soul. Take your time with your drink and spend as much time as you want hanging out at Temperance's bar. When there appears to be nothing left coming down the rainbow bridge, you'll know it is time to leave. Take a few nice deep breaths, say thank you, and carry on with your day.

Wandering

Temperance lands at number fourteen in the major arcana, between Death and the Devil. Her numbers connect her to the Hierophant, since 1 + 4 = 5. This means we have come to another card that brings change through knowledge and understanding, but this time, instead of it being so rigid and formal, it is more intuitive and experimental. Where the Hierophant likes to keep to a strict and ancient code of conduct, Temperance likes to mix things up. Today as you wander around in Temperance's shoes, think about how you can change things around and bring some rainbow energy into your daily habit or routine. Consider taking a different way home. Go down to a shopping center or mall that is new to you. Take a new class or even just say a hello to someone you normally walk straight past during the day. Use the fire energy of this card to get into the "doing" mentality of change. The best adventures are had by those who actively step into them. Temperance says, "Now it's your turn!"

15. THE DEVIL

Demon, temptress, vixen, and scapegoat are just some of the many names that we give to our "get out of jail free," "blame it on everyone else" card, known in the tarot as the Devil. We like to blame the Devil when things go wrong or when a situation makes us look bad in other people's eyes. But in reality, the Devil doesn't make decisions for you, nor does he judge the decisions you do make. If anything, he is an innocent bystander who merely offers up options and alternatives for you to consider. Liking the repercussions of these choices, or deciding whether they are good or bad, is completely irrelevant. The Devil is a results guy, and he does not judge those results. He is not interested in ethics, or morals, or any other man-made judgment. He is just curious to see what happens next. Then again, aren't we all a bit like this? If you look closely at many depictions of the Devil in the tarot you will see a very familiar couple chained and bound at the Devil's feet: the Lovers. The Lovers remind you that you alone made these commitments back at card six. You made your choice, you committed to a path, and now you are paying the price. Nothing is free, everything has a price, and the Devil, being a man of business, is only too happy to come and collect your payment. It may look like the Devil has bound the Lovers, as if he has chained them up to be slaves to their decisions. But in truth they have placed themselves in a subservient position. The Devil is not keeping them there against their will, and if anything, he doesn't care if they stay or leave. Guilt, shame, and fear root the Lovers to the spot. In many spiritual teachings, guilt, shame, doubt, and fear are considered demons, which is an interesting way to look at the Devil card. You could say that the Devil holds a space for you to face your demons, pay your karmic debts, and clear anything that binds you to the past. In this respect, the Devil is not a captor but a liberator, a healer, and a necessary player on the soul's path to enlightenment.

PATHWORK

Intentional

Have you ever heard the phrase "Devil's advocate"? This is the person that feels the need to inform you of everything that could possibly go wrong with your ideas or plans. Most people see this as a bad thing; they will tell you they don't want to give it "energy" or waste mind space on it. I am a big fan of the Devil's advocate. Seriously, I want someone to tell me how it could all go horribly wrong. I want to know the worst thing that could happen so I can release my fear. Fear is a weird and wobbly thing, and not knowing, in my opinion, is far worse than knowing. For as they say, the Devil is in the details. So today, look at those details, all of them. Sit with these possibilities in your meditation, and see them unfold as a passive observer. Don't allow yourself to attach to any of the emotions that bubble up as a result; just watch and learn. Take a few nice deep breaths and hold space for your personal Devil to show up in your meditation. Sit with your Devil and ask what you are missing that could come back to cause you pain and suffering later. Really listen to what your Devil has to say. Remember to breathe through this dialogue and don't react to it. Just take the information. Once your Devil is done giving you the insider's tour to everything that can and possibly will go wrong with your current problem, goal, or project, open your eyes and jot it all down in your journal. These small details will make a huge difference moving forward.

Intuitive

Each of us has an inner Devil, a piece of ourselves that we have created to make us feel bad and to make us suffer. Your job in meditation is to find that creation and liberate yourself from it. This does not necessarily mean killing it or trying to deny its existence. This is about learning to be in control of the narrative and making sure you are intentionally telling the story you want to hear, instead of letting the hurt, wounded pieces of yourself control the story. Liberation is what the Devil is all about. The Devil wants you to be in control and to feel what true power is, but you need to be focused and consistent with your inner work. The next time your butt hits the meditation cushion, bring your Devil card with you. Place it somewhere where you will be able to focus on it, and let it guide you to the place where you inner Devil resides. Observe what games and tricks your inner Devil is playing and start changing the rules. Find the loopholes and learn to play dirty. Just remember, it is all you: the good, bad, and indifferent. It's all you, all the time.

Wandering

A lot of people believe that the Devil likes chaos, and that somehow he thrives when things are out of order. I just don't understand where that line of thinking comes from, as the Devil in the tarot is linked to both Capricorn and Saturn, two of the most organized and disciplined energies of the zodiac and planets. Capricorn is a hardworking business executive that likes to plan and is always looking toward the future. Saturn is the planet of order, structure, rules, and regulation. Does that sound like a planet that likes things to get out of control? Both Saturn and Capricorn are innovative, and they tend to like to make things happen when others would walk away and claim it impossible. Today, start walking in the Devil's business shoes. Look at things you would normally make excuses for and instead just get them done. Look for moments in your day when you can come up with a new and interesting solution to a problem or see if you can find a creative way to create a new income stream in your business or life. Find gaps and leaks in your energy, and plug them up so you stop feeling overwhelmed and drained. See where you can organize your time more effectively and research how habit stacking could increase your productivity. Move through your day with the eyes and ears of a CEO, and let both Capricorn and Saturn show you how to go from excuses to results.

16. THE TOWER

The Tower is not always one of the most appreciated cards within the major arcana. Then again, what do you expect after the Devil? Of course things are going to be shaken up! It is only natural that everything that you thought you knew is going to be called into question. The foundation on which you have laid all of your beliefs, biases, and identities has been questioned, tossed around, and reorganized while you were in the Devil's domain. It makes perfect sense that the world you once built would now come crashing down upon you. If it didn't, we would be concerned. This is good. This is positive. This is progress. This is also one of the first lessons you learn in business. What worked in the beginning won't work when you need to expand. You are not at the beginning of your journey anymore; you are somewhere in the middle. The landscape has changed, and so has the way you see it and experience it. None of us should want to cling to outdated modes of doing or being. We should be constantly rebuilding, upgrading, and restructuring our experience and how we engage with the world around us. Otherwise we will become stagnant and stunted, not to mention we will be out of alignment with the natural flow of our soul's path. The Tower is here to shake you out of your complacency, wake you up from your comfort zone slumber, and put you on alert that you may not have noticed that things within you have shifted and changed. I like to think of this card as the spiritual renovation card. Sometimes you have to take a sledgehammer to old walls and open up a space so that it can get more light.

PATHWORK

Intentional

There is nothing more liberating than working with the Tower card on purpose and using it to give your life a good shake, move things around, and blow up your daily routine. Therefore, before you set your intention and allow the Tower to do its damage, make sure you have come to peace with what is about to happen. Know that it might take time to sort through the rubble and find the bits and pieces that will lay the foundation of your next and new chapter. Now take a couple of nice deep breaths, get comfortable, and visualize your life being given a good shake. Ask for what is false to be pulled down. See the illusions that have been created shatter into a million pieces and be carried away on the wind. Straighten your spine and be sure of your breathwork as each piece of the unwanted rubble is crushed, shattered, and torn away. Breathe and just do your best to relax as the Tower works its magic on your intention. Stay with this visualization for as long as is comfortable. When you are finished, just add the following mantra: "I am capable of rebuilding my life no matter how messy the rubble is."

Intuitive

For the most part, people think of the Tower card as something that happens outside of them and a card that will have an impact on the world they see with their physical eyes. The truth is that the Tower card does the majority of its work in the upside-down position, causing change internally. If the upright version of this card hints at an explosion, then think of the reversed position of this card as an implosion, an act of destruction in a space that cannot be seen with one's physical eyes. Unlike in the intentional section where we were looking for things outside of us to change, this exercise is all about what's going on inside. The Tower card in reverse can be a very healing card. It can be a gift for your body, mind, and soul, and you now have some insight into how to use its energy to assist rather than impede you. For this exercise, settle yourself with a couple of nice deep breaths, and if you need to, close your eyes. Now go ahead and visualize the upside down Tower card at work on your inner landscape, clearing out your outdated beliefs and your negative inner dialogue. Take a nice deep breath and see your false fears tumble to the ground inside you. Keep your breathwork going as you see the flashes of light from the Tower's implosion washing over the inside of your body, clearing out your cells and organs, and leaving in its wake nothing put pure healing light. You may notice tingling as the light from the Tower gives you a good clean. Don't judge it; just let it unfold. When you feel you have had enough of the Tower's healing, take another few deep breaths and bring your focus and attention back to the room you are in. If you want to go further with this in your journal feel free to do so.

Wandering

Do you like visiting ruins of ancient cities and villages, or do you seek out sacred sites that once were points of power in ancient civilizations? In many respects these sorts of activities are the Tower card in its wanderer's shoes. As you walk around the decay and ruin of something that has been forgotten, you are literally walking through the aftermath of a Tower moment—the fallen ideas, hopes, and dreams of a time now lost. The ruins of our world, whether newly urban, sacred, or ancient, all share the same story. They all emanate the same energy. They all belong to the Tower card of the tarot. Have you ever taken the time to sit in the midst of something that has fallen apart and tried to hear the story the rubble is telling?

Your task for this pathwork exercise is to find a local ruin. Make sure it's a safe one, I should add, and go and meditate in it or next to it. If you do not have one close by or the urban ruin you have is unsafe, find a picture of a ruin that interests you and use it as the focal point for this exercise. This exercise is more of a mental wandering, a reflection on what is left behind. Think about what ideas or potential this building once had. Who lived or worked in it, and what did this place mean to them? Think about how this place makes you feel. We don't all feel welcome or at peace when we are amongst the forgotten or the left behind. What emotions does this building or set of ruins bring up for you? This is all the Tower card at work, bursting through and making changes, using the damage and aftermath to heal and expand your current situation.

17. THE STAR

Unlike the Moon and the Sun, the Star represents the many planets, dwarf planets, and asteroids that make up our galaxy. Some are closer to Earth than others, which means some shine brighter in our night skies. The stars look different depending on what hemisphere of the Earth you are standing in. The stars here in the north are different than the stars I saw growing up as a child in the south, which probably explains why I am unable to use them as navigators the way I used to in my twenties. For here in the north there is no Southern Cross guiding me on a long dark road in the middle of nowhere. When some look to the skies they are reminded of all that is beyond our reach. The Star is "out there" and we are "in here" on the Earth. The Star reminds us that we are small and unimportant. Stars can burn out or explode, and no one misses them once they cease to exist. They are not immortal and are very much dependent on the conditions of the universe around them, much like we are.

In this respect, the Star card is a mirror, a reflection of ourselves hurtling through space for a brief moment in infinite time. We get to shine for only the blink of an eye in the memory of space. Our light is quickly eaten by the void that is between all of the other stars floating in the cold, black openness of the universe. So while looking for our favorite star in the night sky can cause us great joy, it can also fill us with great emptiness. The Star in the tarot connects us to the vastness of the universe. It alludes to what else is "out there" and the magic that we are not able to see. For some, this connection pulls them to seek answers via experience, but for the rest, it gives something to dream, write, and paint about. How you work through the pathwork exercises will let you know if you are an explorer or a dreamer.

PATHWORK

Intentional

What if everything you could possibly wish for happens and it all goes right? This is a question I ask myself and my clients all the time. Working with the Star card on purpose lets you work on seeing your wishes and dreams come true. It gives you space to visualize, create vision boards, and focus your thoughts on what steps you will need to take when it all works out for the positive. This also allows you to examine how you feel about things going right. Pull your Star card from your deck, hold it in front of you, and stare into it. As you breathe and gaze at the card, visualize it working its magic on all your heart's desires. See all of your current projects and goals being fulfilled. Watch them in glorious color all playing out in front of your eyes. Magnify these images and make them as vibrant as possible, then slip them into a balloon. Take your balloon and release it into the night sky so it can become one with the Star itself. This quick sixty-second visualization is super powerful and will keep your mind focused and sharp while preparing your emotions for everything to end up exactly the way your heart wants it to. Then if anyone asks, "Well, what if it all goes right?" you can smile and give them your answer.

Intuitive

It is said that we are all made of stardust, and that particles of stars make up our organic bodies. This must mean that when we make a wish, we are really wishing on ourselves. I sometimes wonder if this is why the Star card in the tarot is often associated with healing, because the energy or particle matter of stardust is within our own human bodies. Maybe this is also why we find the Star, like Temperance, playing with water, even though neither of these cards is associated with water. Water is cleansing, it purifies, and it flows, all elements of healing work. So what messages of healing is your inner stardust sending out to you? Let's do a simple three-card spread and find out. First, remove your Star card from your deck and place it faceup in front of you, but leave enough space under it for a row of three cards. Take the remainder of your deck and give it a shuffle. While you shuffle, ask the cards to tell you what healing message your inner stardust wants you to know. Keep shuffling until you feel the cards are ready with their answer, then flip over the first two cards from your deck, as well as the one on the bottom. You should now have your Star card and a row of three faceup cards in front of you. Read the three cards like they are a sentence, each card adding a word or two to the answer to your question. If you want to explore this spread further, pick up your journal and write away.

Wandering

The stars are for wanderers. They guide us, thrill us, offer up mysteries that seek solutions, plant adventure in those who gaze at them, and make others grateful for something safe, secure, and stable to stand on. Wanderers look to the stars, and when they do, they dream. Dreaming is the most powerful pathwork you can do. What star speaks to you? Which of the stars do you stare at and secretly whisper all of your hopes and dreams to? For this exercise you need to wander with your star, the one that fascinates you or the one that you were born under. Just pick a star and claim it as your own. Perhaps it's the morning star (Venus and sometimes Mercury) or the dog star (Sirius). Whichever star is the one you constantly look for, wander with it over the course of the next seven days. Track its path across the sky and log its travels. There are some wonderful apps to help with this. See if your star wanders in a straight line or is more free-roaming. Notice if your star is close to the Earth at this time of year, or if it is harder to spot. Keep a log of the other stars or planets your star hangs out with as well. Let it tell you a story while you tell it your hopes, dreams, and fears. Wander together within the darkness and see if your star is having an impact on your habits and daily flow.

18. THE MOON

The Moon comes before the Sun, just as day follows night. They are partners in a dance of light and dark. This ongoing dance around the Earth provides us with a sense of time, an illusion of order, and a form of measurement. We measure days, months, seasons, and years by the partnership between the sun and the moon, yet the moon seems to be the one that terrifies people the most, for it has long been associated with secrets, monsters, demons, and unknown threats.

Why is it that these things only seem to come out in the dark? This is something I have always wondered, because it's not as if bad things never happen when the sun is shining and the sky is a brilliant blue. People can be just as terrified during the day as they can at night. So why does the domain of the moon get such a bad rap? Could it be that our ancestors just didn't like the way the dark blinded them to danger? Or is it that one too many storytellers has brainwashed us all with tales of things that go bump in the night?

There is no doubt that when the moon is out, the world in which we navigate our journey does look different. However, different is not automatically bad, and in many ways, we learn more through differences than sameness. If anything, the moon is more revealing than it is concealing. For in the light, things can get lost, forgotten, and ignored, but under the watchful gaze of our lunar ally, these same things will move around thinking they are protected by the wrapping darkness of night. This is where you will find the things that you think you have lost. This is where you will be able to align to solutions that hide themselves amongst your daily to-do list. It is under the moon that you can drop your social mask and be your true self. If there really are any monsters who live in the moonlight, then I suggest it is the true version of who we are, our true self that we only get glimpses of when the moon is full. Perhaps this is why the darkness and the moonlight scare so many, because they don't want to see the truth of who they are.

PATHWORK

Intentional

For this exercise, let's focus on two of the moon's phases: the new moon and the full moon. As the new moon begins to fill, it is a perfect time to work on manifesting energy. As we look to the moon and see it filling, so too do we look to our wallets, hearts, fridges, cupboards, and minds and see them filling as well. Then, once the moon has its fill and bursts forth during the full moon, we start to give thanks. Between the full moon and new moon is a fabulous time for gratitude work. Thank it for filling all the corners of your life. This very simple moon practice will do wonders for your life, as it will get you out of your head and into a more organic, flowing rhythm with nature and the planets. Far too often we allow ourselves to get caught up in our heads, thinking we know how things work and how they should flow. But the truth is everything has its own flow, its own way of showing up, and its own sense of timing. Working with these two phases of the moon grounds your manifestation energy, gives it purpose, and provides a ritual, which is something we could all do with a little more of.

Intuitive

Do you keep a dream journal? And I don't mean the type where you record your nighttime dreams. I mean the kind where you write down your goals, your wishes … you know—the real dreams. If you don't, think about starting one and sleeping with it under your pillow. This simple nighttime ritual will help you stay connected to your dreams, goals, and wishes. Start by removing your Moon card from your deck and placing it beside your bed. You don't have to be able to see it while you're lying down, but it is nice if you can. Give yourself an extra ten to fifteen minutes before you turn your light off or pick up your nightly book to read. Use this time to open your dream journal and make a few notes or entries. This could be marking off things that you have done to move toward this goal. Or maybe just daydreaming about being inside your dream. It really doesn't matter what you do, as long as it is positive, upbeat, and adds good energy to your dream. When you are finished with your entries, place your dream journal under your pillow. Lay your head on your pillow and close your eyes, then take a couple of nice deep breaths and say the words "I love you, moon, thank you, moon, for making my dreams come true" a couple of times. That's it! A simple dreamy nighttime ritual.

Wandering

Whether it is sunrise or sunset, I love walking when the moon is out and the animals, insects, and birds of the night have come out to play. It is literally a different world. The sounds are different, the smells are different, and your eyes see things differently. Wandering around under the light of the moon, in the cooler air of the night or the early morning, can be incredibly healing. It can calm the mind and the body at the same time without you even having to think about it. Just move your feet, get lost in the moon's environment, and boom, instant stress relief. The very act of being outside under the moon waiting for the stars to come out is a contemplative process, especially if you can leave your phone and all other digital devices inside. Taking time to move through your garden, stretching out in your backyard, or wandering along the shoreline at the beach are some of the best interactive pathworking practices I can recommend. They not only ground you, but put you in a receptive and reflective mood. I have often taken my Moon card outside and propped it up while I sat and watched the moon make its way into the night sky. I have kept it with me as I watched one set of birds gather together in the trees to sleep, while another got ready to explore the night. I have placed it in my back pocket as I have strolled by the beach, gone to a night market, or just hiked through some nighttime trails. The Moon reminds us that in many respects we live in two very active and different worlds—one that happens when the sun is shining and one that happens when most of us are sleeping. Go and explore the world under the Moon's watch. See what magic it has on display, and allow yourself to get lost in a world that is similar yet different from the one you habitually know.

19. THE SUN

The sun is one of the few elements that is required for life. Maybe that is why so many sacred texts talk about how in the beginning, there was light. Without the sun, things would not grow. As humans, we also have a connection and need for the vitamin-D-rich light the sun gives us. Our bones would literally crumble and fail to keep us upright without the vitamins the sun provides. There is no doubt that on a cold winter's day, seeing the sun fills one with joy, warmth, and life. However, in summer, our relationship to the sun can be a little more complicated. There are those of you who are true sun bunnies and don't fully thrive until the heat of the sun hits your skin, and then there are those of us who prefer gentler light and find it stifling, suffocating, and confining during the summer months. Which one of these you are will dictate the terms of your relationship with this card. The sun does not just bring warmth, however; it also brings light. It graces our lives with extended periods of illumination, times when we find ourselves out of the shadows and darkness and in the reality of the world that we have created. Our relationships with light and heat are not one and the same. They are two very separate elements within the Sun card. I am a fan of the light and notice my moods are elevated when there are blue skies and a glowing sun; however, I am not a fan of the heat. Needless to say, this makes *my* personal relationship with the Sun complicated, and yours may be as well. Regardless of your relationship with the Sun, it will magnify and heat up the cards around it, so notice what and where it shines its light. You may not want the full blast of the sun on you, but you may be grateful for the other things it brings out of the shadows. All in the sun's path shall be blessed with light, even if they don't want it. Take a good look around when the sun is out and see what you may have missed hiding in the dark corners and spaces of both your inner and outer worlds.

PATHWORK

Intentional

Let's talk about light. Light is something many spiritual seekers discuss. They talk about finding the light, being the light, embracing the light and working with the light. This always sounds like a lot of work to me. The sun is all nonstop, continuous light, and it has a way of bursting forth every single morning without much effort, just because of the nature of what it is. Maybe there is a very distinct lesson in that for all of us. Be more and chase less, and more light will naturally be able to burst forth. As you take your Sun card and place it in front of you, think about things you are trying to push into being or that you're working too hard to control.

Now pick up your deck, minus the Sun card, and give the cards a shuffle. When you feel you have shuffled enough, place the cards facedown in front of you and fan them out. Now find the one card that seems to light up. I know this sounds a little out there, but trust the energy of the Sun to guide you and show you the path to more grace and ease. Just let your gaze roam over the cards until one of them lights up, or at the very least appears lighter than all the other cards. Pair this card with your Sun card and read them as one answer to this question: How do I allow the light to move through me without me forcing it or trying to be in control? If you wish to go deeper, pick up your journal and see what else these two cards have to say.

Intuitive

I know this isn't discussed a lot when it comes to the Sun card in tarot, but like the suit of wands, the Sun burns. It is pure, raw fire that has the potential for mass destruction. Light brings life, fire takes life. This is a useful tool to use during meditation, because you can use the fiery energy of the sun to burn away thoughts, feelings, and patterns of behavior you no longer want, and use the sun's light to grow new thoughts, feelings, and habits in their place. Working with the Sun card during meditation can be both healing and liberating. Place your Sun card where you can see it, as you take some nice deep breaths. Visualize the Sun in its natural form as a burning ball of gas, flaring powerfully in the darkness of space. As you breathe and focus, think about feelings, situations, and difficulties you want the Sun to burn away. See these things being pulled into the Sun and destroyed instantly. Keep this up until you feel you have nothing left to give to the Sun for now. Now allow the Sun to send you healing prana to cleanse your body. Perhaps give this healing energy a color and watch it flow out of the Sun and into your body. When you feel complete, restored, and light, take some more deep breaths and bring yourself to the present moment. Do this small meditation as often as you like. If you feel drawn to do so, journal about your experiences with the Sun as a point of mediation and release.

Wandering

Are you a sunrise or a sunset type of person? I'm a sunrise person. I love that time of the day because it is cooler and quieter than any other time. This is also one of my most productive times as well. There is just something so very magical to me about sunrises. My wife, on the other hand, is a sunset person. She loves watching the sun go down, especially over the ocean. She comes alive at dusk and marvels at what she calls the golden hour. This is how each of us pays homage to sun. Some of us do it in the morning, as it peeks over the horizon and sheds its light on the promise of a new day, while others do it in the evenings, thanking the sun for all that has unfolded in the now ending day. These times of day are important, as they align the sun with two very distinct directions, east and west. Directions are essential to the wanderer and each has a lesson and a meaning. East is the direction of birth and all things new, including possibilities and opportunities, while west is the direction of the ancestors and endings, of things that have once been, but are not forgotten. If you are a sunrise person, then the sun has more of an impact on you as you start new projects, and you feel more of a buzz of energy when you begin things. If you are more of a sunset person, then the west is your direction and you enjoy seeing things come together and you revel in the end result. You will probably be more inclined to connect with ritual and prayer that deals with ancestors and stories and ideas that have been passed down. For this exercise, you are being asked to connect with your sun energy direction—be it east with the sunrise or west with the sunset—see what lessons and messages this direction has for you, and become more aligned with your sun power to know what facets of the Sun card serve you best.

20. JUDGEMENT

If there really is a higher divine power that could rid you of all of your sins, would you want that? Would you want to be rid of all of your guilt, shame, and regret, and if so, would you truly be able to let it go? The card of Judgement offers you such a deal. It is the card that wipes the slate clean and absolves you of anything that you had to do to get to this point in your journey. It basically tells you that all is forgiven, so please move on and complete what you started. But how many of us can actually let go of the hungry ghosts of the past that easily? In Buddhism, guilt and shame are considered sins—sins that if left to fester will create demons and monsters for the mind to fight, teaching us that all judgment happens within the mind only. Carrying around any past ghosts wreaks havoc with our ability to make life-affirming decisions. These mental wounds slow you down and leave the door wide open for another demon—fear—to walk in. When we finally release our need to judge and be judged, we close the door on fear and starve it of light once and for all. The Judgement card offers you a path to peace and enlightenment. It shows you what can be achieved when you let the past go and allow yourself to be reborn. This is something that happens to us all as we go through one ego death after another. You may have killed off part of the ego mind back in the Death card, but up until now you have been holding onto the guilt of wanting and needing change in your life. We have all been there—wondering if the decisions we have made for our own growth and expansion were worthwhile, especially when they seemed to cause others some sort of pain and suffering, even if we know there was no other choice our soul self could have made. It is no mistake that we must pass through the land of Judgement before we are allowed to make our way to the World card. In other words, we cannot end our journey without first forgiving ourselves for taking it in the first place.

Intentional

The Judgement card connects us to the act of forgiveness. Forgiveness is never about another person. It is all about ourselves, making it one of the most powerful forms of healing. The act of forgiveness is an intentional act of self-love. It happens when we stop seeing ourselves as broken victims and start seeing ourselves as perfectly imperfect humans. Humans are messy. They make mistakes; they have a knack for causing great suffering and tend to turn this on themselves in cruel and creative ways. Yet despite it all, humans have an incredible capacity to love, hope, and forgive.

Today you will meditate on forgiving yourself. Start with something small and slowly work your way up to the bigger things. We beat ourselves up about small, petty things all the time, so start there. Take a few nice deep breaths and say, "I forgive myself for ..." and fill in the blank. You can close your eyes if you feel drawn to do so. For me it is often "I forgive myself for speaking badly to myself," or "I forgive myself for setting unrealistic expectations," or "I forgive myself for being angry when it only added to the problem." I think you get the idea. I have always been amazed at how just working on the small stuff has massive ripple effects with the big stuff, so feel free to keep your forgiveness meditations small. The important thing is to do them often, at least a couple of times a week. They only take a couple of minutes. Do it in the shower, in the bath, while you are stuck in traffic. Just breathe, forgive, and release.

Intuitive

Imagine a world where everyone is forgiven and loved completely and wholly for who and what they are; a world where each person's heart chakra is so big and so strong that it can see nothing but pure unconditional love for themselves and all those around them. I know this sounds like a mythical world, but this is the energy of the Judgement card. As archangel Gabriel blows the horn of God, she literally wipes the slate clean for all of those who have risen for another chance at life. It is interesting that we find this card near the end of the major arcana, at the end of the road, at the edge of the World. It's as if you need to learn to drop everything you have carried with you on your journey before you can finally make it to that warm embrace waiting for you in the arms of the Mother and the arms of the World card. As you meditate on this card, think about what it would mean to be able to open your heart that wide, to be able to love that purely, and to be able to see yourself as perfect and without shame. As you meditate or do a yoga pose, visualize all of your pain, all of your anger, all of your perceived failures just being blown away by a loving angel, leaving you naked, exposed, and raw. See yourself dressed in new skin and swelling with the beat of a new and more divine heart. With each inhale, focus on drawing Gabriel's energy into your heart center, and with each exhale, push out all identities, tags, and boxes you have tried to fit yourself into. See how working with the Judgement card in this way makes you lighter and brighter, and gives you a sense of new and renewed hope for the future.

Wandering

The Judgement card can symbolize an awakening, an expansion in consciousness, and a rebirth of ourselves. This makes sense considering its placement in the major arcana, for none of us makes it out of an experience the same as we were when we went in. It just stands to reason that we would see a new version of ourselves reflected back to us as we get ready to cross the finish line. In this respect, the Judgement card shows our butterfly phase. Having broken through our cocoon in the light of the Sun, we now emerge here in the Judgement card to walk into the World. We all have butterfly moments, and now it would seem you have come to yours. Use this card to seek out the parts of you that have gone through a transformation. Find places that no longer look or feel the same to you as they did three months, twelve months, or two years ago. Even the way you navigate through the world around you is different, but have you really taken the time to notice this?

As you make your way through your world in this newly birthed butterfly body, notice if sounds seem louder or quieter or if your sense of smell is sharper or duller. Seeing how you engage with space, negotiate environments, and experience places will be the best way to truly live the transforming, rebirthing energy that the Judgement card brings you. Go and wander. Take your wings for a test drive and see just how different the world around you feels, looks, sounds, and smells.

21. THE WORLD

Within the major arcana, this is the last card or last stop in the Fool's journey. The Fool has progressed through all of the cards of the major arcana, growing, learning, and evolving along the way. Once at the World card, the Fool is changed and no longer the same. The Fool is now more evolved and possibly even more enlightened. In this respect, the World card represents completion, the end of a cycle, journey, or quest. There is no going back once you have made it this far. The only option is to start again. This is the natural progression of cycles: you begin, you end, and you begin again. Each time you begin, you start as a new and different person. Who have you become? What sort of person are you now that you have made it through your journey or quest? Are things as you had expected them to be? What does the world look like through your wiser, more enlightened eyes?

We never come out of a situation the same as we went in, just as the caterpillar does not come out of its cocoon the same. You are now the butterfly, transformed and changed yet still you. One of the elements that is not discussed often with the World card is the notion of stillness. Before you wander too far, you may want to take a breath and just observe the landscape for a while. Things are different where you now find yourself, and you have to figure out the best way to navigate around this new world. You may not even be sure how you fit into the landscape you now find yourself in. Just be still. Sit for a while and slow yourself down.

PATHWORK

Intentional

So now you may think you are finished. You think you have come full circle, and now you get to just enjoy the world you have created. Are you sure it is not missing anything? For this exercise, take the World card from your deck and place it faceup with the image upside down in front of you. Now pick up the remaining cards in your deck and give them a shuffle. When you have shuffled enough, take the card from the top of the deck and the card from the bottom of the deck and place them faceup under your upside down World card. The card from the top of the deck shows what needs to be taken care of before you can turn your World card back to its upright position. The card from the bottom of the deck shows what needs to be left behind, as it has no place in this new world you have created. You can journal with these two cards if you find it helpful. Keep your World card upside down. Do not turn it back to the upright position until you have taken care of what is shown in the card you pulled from the top of your deck. Only then will you be ready to embrace the World and all the wonderful things you have created within it.

Intuitive

When you hear the saying "The world is yours to take," what do you think of? Does the statement overwhelm you, excite you, terrify you, or sadden you? In business, the talking heads and so-called gurus are always screaming that people are scared of success, that it is not failure but success that makes people choke, self-sabotage, and blow shit up. These are all things to ponder as the tarot literally hands you the World. This gives us something to work through in our meditation practice, especially thinking about which parts of the world bring us joy, which parts bring us sadness, which parts we embrace and accept, and which parts we choose to deny. As you bring the World card into your meditation practice, contemplate the idea of taking the world, holding it in your arms, and claiming it. Claim it for healing. Take a nice deep breath and think about all the times you have talked yourself out of something that would have made you feel successful and happy. Shift the moments of pain, doubt, and fear out of your heart, and exhale them back out into the world as raw energy just waiting to be transformed into something amazing. Repeat this until you feel lighter and less overwhelmed. When you feel complete you may let go of the world. Place it back into space. Watch how claiming and healing yourself will in turn heal the world around you. Go on now and take the world; it is yours, you have earned it.

Wandering

The World card is the reminder of the dirt under our shoes, the grass between our toes, the rain on our face, the wind in our hair, and the sun on our skin. It connects us to our five senses and grounds us in an experience that can only ever be experienced right here, right now, on this planet. It is easy in our busy daily lives to forget these things, and to disconnect ourselves from the elements that make this world our home, albeit a temporary one.

Just for today, connect with the world. Instead of worrying about your to-do list, stop and feel the wind, the sun, or the rain. Instead of rushing from one appointment to the next, sit, take a breath, and marvel at the ground beneath you and the sky above you. Give thanks to the gravity that stops you from being sucked out into space, and show some gratitude to the planet that puts up with you and your moods every day until your organic vessel gives out. Observe your immediate world, including the people, the animals, the experiences, the emotions, and anything else that you have deemed important to you. Have you created a world that brings you joy or is it one that makes you feel trapped? The World card is not just an ending, the completion of a journey started twenty-one cards ago; it is a reminder of the stage on which your journey has taken place, a stage that you will get to dance on until your dance shoes no longer fit. Therefore, wander through your world with a grateful heart and a thankful mind. Bless every leaf, every bug, and every crack in the pavement, because this world has supported you, and it will continue to do so as long as it turns.

3

. . . .

THE COURT CARDS

THE SIXTEEN COURT CARDS, regardless of which school of tarot your cards belong to, tend to represent developmental stages or steps in a process. They show a very distinct learning curve, from apprentice or beginner—the Pages—to the initiated and in constant training—the Knights—to the networker, social developer, and change agent—the Queens—to the Master—the Kings. This approach also negates the gender often ascribed to each of these cards. Getting rid of the gender element in this process is probably one of the more liberating ways to work with these cards, as now we are focused on where we find ourselves in a cycle, stage, process, or goal instead of whether or not we need to be more masculine or feminine. This is why this section has been written with nonbinary pronouns. Each deck creator designs their cards around the energy that calls to them from the deck itself. It is not in any way meant to limit or control how you interact with the cards or the characters portrayed on them. Regardless of what gender is pictured on the court cards themselves, each one still represents a stage you will enter along your path. For me this is truly helpful, especially when I am working on long-term goals or short-term experiences, which, by the way, is a distinction you will need to understand before you begin your pathwork with the court cards. Are you focusing on something long term (perhaps with a timeline of three to five years) or something that is a short-term experience (taking perhaps three to twelve months)? The time frame is important, as it lets you know how quickly you will need to work through each of the court card stages. Perhaps you will find you're further along than you first thought, and those five years just got reduced to two!

Let me give you a couple examples of what I mean and show you how you can set up your pathwork experience with the court cards to supercharge your goals, manifestations, or healing processes.

For the first example, let's look at something that is long term. Because I work with a lot of female entrepreneurs, we'll use the idea of starting a business. This needs to be something that you plan to grow over a three- to five-year period. If you can't commit to a business for three years, then just don't do it. Business is hard; it takes a lot of time and a lot of single-minded focus and concentration, which is why you have to commit the time, and lots of it. For the sake of this argument, let's say you are planning to hit King status in three years. This means in three years time you will be considered an expert in your field and a true leader in your industry. People well seek you out because of your expertise. This is a fabulous goal, but how do you get there? Well, by starting at the beginning, of course. Hello, Pages!

You want to spend as much time in this stage as possible. You need to surrender to the energy of this stage, not rush through it.

I see boredom kill so many businesses. Everyone is in a rush to be King. Don't be. It's hard at the top and even harder if you didn't learn all the right lessons in the beginning. This stage with the Pages sets the foundation for everything else that comes next. You literally build upward from the foundation you lay in this stage. Love yourself and your business enough to build a strong, stable, and secure foundation, and only when that is done should you move on to the next stage, the Knights.

The Knights, in many respects, kick up the active energy of the process or phase you are in. Unlike the Pages, who are more observational and focused on single tasks, the Knights are where the action really revs up. The Knights need to hone multiple skills, juggle multiple responsibilities, and manage a wide variety of tasks in short periods of time. In many respects, the Knights represent first level management of your business. The Knight will actively engage you on all the elements of your business—setting up email lists, taking ideas from the Pages phase and turning them into real tangible things, creating a social media presence, blogging or vlogging, and hiring a virtual assistant, just to name a few. Under the watchful eye of the Knights, you will learn product creation skills and battle plans, also known as launch strategies. You will sharpen your mind, learn to limit your distractions, use boredom as a creative weapon, and become singularly focused on the long-term goal of becoming King of your domain. You will find that you go through many Knight phases on the path toward your goals. Like the Pages, you never really say goodbye to this stage; rather you just learn when to actively engage in this phase and when to move on to the next one, which would be the Queens.

The Queens bring with them all the glitz and glamour you would expect, but don't let that fool you. If you have made it to this level, you are working harder than you ever have before. The only difference is that you are enjoying it. You are so engaged with what you are doing that it no longer feels like work but more like an extension of who you are. You may have seen some sparks of success while you were in the Knight's phase, but you haven't seen anything like what you will see here at the executive branch of the tarot court cards. In many respects, this is the make-or-break stage of your journey. Things will come at you fast, and you won't have the time you wish you had to spend on dreaming and creating. The pace at this level can overwhelm people. It may have been what you said you wanted, but now that you are here, the pressure to constantly keep up, keep creating, keep moving, and keep relevant is starting to get you down. It is when working with the Queens that you will either give up and bow out or learn how to use this pressure to create something miraculous. There are many people, myself included, who would love to stay right here at this stage. There is something so satisfying about getting this phase right. It makes you forget why you ever wanted to be King. The problem is that you will end up at King level by default, just because you are such an awesome, badass Queen. Unfortunately, that is just the way it goes, so like it or not, you are about to level up.

Believe it or not, being King isn't anywhere near as much fun as people dream it is. Those who have gotten this far know that wearing this particular crown is hard. Now more than ever, the responsibility lies solely at your feet. Things you could get away with before are now frowned upon and called out, often in public. Once you have stepped foot into this fourth stage or phase, all eyes are squarely on you. Everyone wants to know you, know what you are doing, who you are with, what you are wearing or eating, you name it. You are the King and people know who you are. Of course, this was the goal all along, to be King of your field, career, niche, and business in three years. But now that you are at the top, now that you have worked through all of the phases ... now what?

That is just a simple example of how to use the court cards as steps, stages, and phases. This allows them to become more focused concepts for your pathwork practice. Now let's see how this plays out in a smaller goal over a much tighter time frame.

Again, let's stick to a business framework. Let's say you just signed up as an essential oil advocate. You love essential oils and you truly want to share this passion with as many people as possible, so you have set yourself a goal of reaching the Elite sales title in your first year. Since you now have your goal, you would settle in with the Pages and start studying. Learn your oils and gather as much information as you can about how to use the oils, market the oils, and close a sale. Ask lots of questions of people who have already done what you want to achieve. After you have gathered all the data you need, you would move into the action phases and start being known as an essential oil advocate. This is when you would start posting on your blog and social media sites about the oils you love and use on a regular basis. You would start crunching your numbers and really pay attention to the questions others now ask you. Next you would move into the Queens stage by finding other people to collaborate with, and you might see if you can get on some podcasts, or start one of your own. You may write guest blog pieces and see about joining other groups that are a natural fit for your product, or looking into what partnerships and joint ventures you can create. The Queens love to network, so think about how you can start classes or create a meet-up group, or even get yourself to a conference or event that puts you face-to-face with others. If you have done all of this correctly and with a committed, focused mind, you should reach your goal of being the Elite King by the end of the year. Or who knows—maybe you will do even better than that and your results will blow you away. Before you know it, you will be the almighty leader of your own team of hopeful advocates who now dream of being where you are, and guess what? You can tell them all about how you used the tarot court cards to track and plot your goal of going from Page to King in under twelve months! Hurray!

I could write these examples for pretty much anything—weight loss, health and well-being, relationships, you name it. The same stages, phases, and steps apply. There is literally nothing you cannot achieve by following the stages of the tarot court cards. Now that you have seen what is possible with these cards, let's take a deeper dive into the individuals that make these sixteen cards so special, because getting to know the energies of these phases, steps, and processes will only empower you and your goals more.

PAGES

The Pages are, in many respects, a representation of someone who is just learning to meditate. They are beginning a journey with a very specific destination in mind. For a Page, the goal is to be a Knight, and for the newbie meditator, it is time to either reduce stress, increase one's level of awareness, improve one's mental focus and clarity, or, for some, reach enlightenment. The Pages and the beginner meditator both start off exactly the same way: by learning how to become expert observers. The newbie meditator, or for the sake of this book, the newbie pathworker, is learning how to observe their thoughts, feelings, actions, and material existence. The Pages break these components up over four cards, which makes working with the Pages a fabulous tool for new meditators and pathworkers alike. I will often get my healing clients to start working with the Page cards in the tarot as part of their healing journey, especially after an intense few months of healing work. This is to ground the new energy that is rising inside of them, and to assist them in making better decisions and taking more aligned actions for their health and well-being goals. The Pages are the very first steps in a much longer journey, but before they even begin that journey, they need to put in the time and do the slow tedious work of getting their bodies, minds, emotions, and spirits aligned with the experience itself.

The Page of Swords is the starting point for mental training. This Page must observe the thoughts, beliefs, biases, and words of those around them. Much like a baby learns how to speak, what to believe, and how to be prejudiced, the Page of Swords finds themselves in a world where they have to relearn all they thought they knew. It is here in the Page of Swords that we start to understand that truth, in and of itself, may be more fluid then we are willing to admit. Just as you learn how to meditate, the Page of Swords must also learn to observe the thoughts that float around in their head. They must examine, without judgment, their inner dialogue, and see how it matches or doesn't match the dialogue of those around them. They must also learn to do this without attachment. The Page of Swords is only an observer at this stage. Even though they may wish to swing that sword all on their own, the consequences of doing so will cause more harm than good.

The Page of Wands is the first time we have been asked to monitor how we might act or react to the world around us. As babies, we learn how to act and react from our parents. Their triggers often become our triggers in one form or another. The way we deal with fight or flight becomes less instinctive and more habitual the older we get, showing that we learn how to act or react to triggers over the course of our human lives. Here in the Page of Wands, you are being asked to put all of that under the microscope. Becoming the observer of our actions and reactions is actually harder than monitoring our thoughts. If you have ever undertaken any new habit training, you will know exactly how hard this is. The Page of Wands is a crucial card in habit changing, for if you cannot first observe how you interact and engage in the world around you, you can't change it either. Think about things you have wanted to change in your life, like bad habits you tried to break or new habits you have tried to create. How easy was it to do any of that? Research shows us that the older we get, the harder it is to change habitual behavior, yet it doesn't say it can't be done. You just have to make a decision to do it, and then walk that journey. Lucky for you, you have the Page of Wands to assist you. Of course, the Page of Wands has a bit of swagger and cockiness about them, but at some point, self-preservation will kick in, and if you can stick with the tedious task of being the ever-present observer in your reactionary world, you will see your focus, clarity, and resolve grow stronger and better with each passing day.

The Page of Cups introduces us to the consequences of our dreams, feelings, emotions, and imagination. Not unlike the Page of Wands, the Page of Cups needs to be on alert for things that trigger them. The watery energy of the cups is a challenging energy to work with at the best of times, but it is even harder when you cannot do anything but sit on the shore and watch. This act of looking or observing is actually seen in many Rider-Waite-Smith decks, as the Page of Cups is the only Page that has their own animal totem with them: the fish. I am not going to go into a discussion here about the fish and what it symbolizes, but you can check out my book *Tarot Court Cards for Beginners* if you want to go further with the fish. For now, let's just say the fish and the Page offer us up the complex duology of emotional energy. It is both internal and external. It flows in us, through us, and out of us. What emotional conditions we create internally shape the physical conditions of the world around us. The Page of Cups is learning that in order to understand their emotions better, they will also need to learn how to observe the reflection of that energy in the world they engage in. This means tapping into that other lovely cup's energy: intuitive sight. Seeing via the third eye while still keeping the physical eyes open is one of the hardest things for new meditators to do. In fact, it is hard even when you have been meditating for many years, but this is where it all begins, right here in the Page of Cups with the ever-watchful fish. The watcher and the watched are both taking notes and exploring how their feelings shape the world, one emotion at a time.

The Page of Pentacles deals with pretty much everything in the physical material world, including all the things you can feel, taste, and touch. This is the Page of material resources, that which makes up the physical world of matter. This Page learns early on in the game of life that money is not the only way to be wealthy, and that most forms of abundance have nothing to do with money at all. The Page of Pentacles also learns just how closely our bodies, health, and food are linked to our beliefs about abundance. This Page doesn't have time for delving deep into their emotions, nor do they have time to sit around and contemplate their navels, oh no, because while others are off wondering about the meaning of life, the Page of Pentacles is learning what makes the world turn and how they can move, flow, and grow right alongside it. Walking hand in hand with the Page of Pentacles, you will learn just how interconnected the physical world actually is. The Page spends each and every day collecting data, finding patterns, and seeing how things connect. The Page is, after all, training to be a Knight, but in order to get to that status there is much to master. The Page is learning about their body as well, and seeing how it changes, grows, and reacts. The Page of Pentacles is the perfect card to work with when you start a healing journey. Of all of the Pages, this one might be the one that stretches some of your current beliefs, which makes this card a perfect journeying partner.

PATHWORK

Intentional

For this exercise, you will need to pull all four of your Pages out of your deck. Line them up in the following order: pentacles, swords, cups, and wands. Then go ahead and set your intention for some issue, problem, or concern you are currently having with your health or physical body. I recommend writing this intention out and placing it above the four Page cards you've laid out in front of you. You can also set some crystals there and light a candle if you feel moved to do so. In this exercise we are going to be using the Page of Pentacles as a grounding point, mainly because this young Page represents the physical, material world. Take three nice deep breaths in through the nose and out through the mouth and allow yourself to gently relax. Keep your gaze on the Pages as you repeat the following text:

Today I walk hand in hand with the Page of Pentacles to take stock of all my healthy, life-affirming habits. I document and record these things so I can best keep track of them. (Pause)

I ask the Page of Swords to monitor my thoughts, beliefs, and communication surrounding my health intention. May this Page show me where I am out of alignment and where I am communicating correctly about my health and well-being.

I ask the Page of Cups to monitor my feelings and emotions about my current state of health and well-being, and to alert me when my feelings are out of alignment with my current set of health goals.

I ask the Page of Wands to work with the Page of Cups so that I can be intuitively guided to healthy foods, healthy thoughts, healthy people, and nourishing conversations.

I know by walking with the Pages I will be able to better navigate my health and well-being goals.

Take another deep breath and close your eyes; if you feel moved to, picture your intention as being fully fulfilled. Smile as you visualize this completed intention, so that you fill it with positive energy. Take two more nice deep breaths and release the visualization. If you want to, you can keep the cards out, along with any crystals you have used, and leave everything set up until your candle burns down.

Intuitive

One of the hardest lessons for a Page to learn is discipline. It is not in a child's nature to sit still for long. Your own inner child energy gets restless when it is not being stimulated, or when it is being stifled and contained. In this exercise, you get to take the shackles off and let one or all four of the Pages out to roam wild. Take a nice deep breath, settle your body and your mind, and slowly bring up a mental image of yourself as a small child. Once you see yourself in your child image, see if you can figure out which sort of Page you are. What does your energy feel like? Take another nice deep breath and allow your mind to drift to a time when you were fully focused, when your child self was happy, content, and immersed in a task. Hold this scene in your mind's eye for as long as possible. Make it bright and colorful. Enlarge it so it takes up all of your vision. When you feel you have memorized all the joyful elements you can, take another deep breath and write down in your journal any additional information you have about this memory or the task that kept you so still and focused.

Wandering

Pull all four Pages out of your deck and place them facedown in front of you. Close your eyes, scan the cards, and then select the one you get an intuitive hit from (this could be the card that feels warmer or cooler than the others) and turn it over. Whichever Page you have selected is the one that you need to work with today, so go ahead and put the other three Pages back in your deck. This exercise is more about learning how to make a deeper connection with your Page card. Now think about how you would plan a day's worth of activities for this Page. What places would this Page like to visit and what sort of adventures would this Page find the most alluring? If you have the Page of Pentacles, there is a good chance something outside in the backyard or at the local park might be of interest. If you selected the Page of Wands, think more creative and action-based activities, like painting or paintball. If you selected the Page of Cups, perhaps a trip to the library or the beach would be in order. And lastly, if you selected the Page of Swords, maybe a museum or comic book store might be the way to go. Once you have mapped out what you consider your ideal day for your Page, consider going to do all of those activities. You pulled this Page for a reason, maybe because it's time to walk in this Page's shoes for a while.

KNIGHTS

Before we begin this section, I just want to let you know that some of what you are about to read may sound very similar to what you just read in the Page's section. That is because it is. Pages are in training to be Knights, and they overlap in many and various ways. The real difference here is action over observation. Where the Page was more of an active observer, collecting data and then seeing how it applied to the path they found themselves taking, the Knights are action-oriented. This is where the rubber meets the road. This is where things get very, very real. Alright, glad we had this little chat before you dive in, but now it's time to continue.

The Knights are where your thoughts, feelings, and beliefs become action-based habits. These habits will then dictate how you engage with the world around you. Habits are nothing but internalized learned behaviors and things we have programmed into our minds and bodies over extended periods of time. Slowing down, being more aware, and really being present with your thoughts, feelings, actions, and reactions are not easy tasks. But it is essential to attaining a more joyful, healthy, and abundant life. Pathworking with the Knights is a step in the right direction when it comes to creating and maintaining new, life-honoring habits. Here you can train your skills right alongside them. Learn how to be more mindful with the Knight of Swords. Learn how to tap into your emotions and use them to empower you with the Knight of Cups. Learn how to stop being reactive and plan your moves with precise action with the Knight of Wands. And of course, learn how to be in the world of material things but not a part of it with the Knight of Pentacles. Let the next phase of your mindfulness training begin.

The Knight of Swords carries on the lessons that they started learning back when they were a Page. Now, however, it is time to really dig deep and focus like never before. The Knight of Swords knows how important it is to create a calm and focused mind, for this is imperative in battle. When the mind is overcome with fear and self-doubt, one can become a target. However, when the mind is calm, it can make quick and decisive actions that will benefit not only the Knight themselves but all of those that surround them. There is more at stake when one becomes a Knight. This is no longer the journey of one, the single journey of the Page; this is where one person's journey becomes an integral part of other people's stories. This level of responsibility is something the Knight of Swords takes very seriously, which is why you will find this Knight meditating for hours on end, morning, noon, and night. Focus, flow, and awareness are key to this Knight's success. Working with the Knight of Swords will bring you to a quieter, more peaceful state of being. This Knight will show you how to still your mind, expand all of your senses and use what is around you to your advantage. Just don't be fooled into thinking that this Knight is passive. Every action this Knight takes causes a reaction, and they know only too well in which direction that energy will flow and what sort of ripples it will create. This Knight means business and won't take too kindly to anyone thinking they can half-ass their lessons with them. That sword the Knight yields is sharp, and they are not afraid to cause some pain if they feel it's necessary. Therefore, think carefully before you choose to walk with the Knight of Swords and remember that humility will be your longest-serving friend.

The Knight of Wands seriously wants to light a fire under your ass. This Knight has no interest in your excuses and won't take no for an answer. This Knight will never understand why people stand still, nor will this Knight understand why people are afraid of the word *no*, or why others think failure is such a big deal. As far as the Knight of Wands is concerned, you will never truly know anything unless you do it, which is wise, to be honest. Far too often we play out ridiculous scenarios in our heads to convince ourselves to never ask that question, never take that first step, never try changing, never … you can fill in the blank. The Knight of Wands doesn't comprehend this sort of limited thinking. The fiery potential this Knight burns with stops them from ever thinking that they cannot do something. How liberating is that? How different would your life be if you just did all the things your heart desired for you to do? What would your life look like? How different would you feel about who you are and your place in the world? According to this Knight, there are only two types of people: those who do and those who bitch about those who do. The Knight of Wands doesn't listen to people who only complain or only have negative things to say. This Knight takes that sort of toxic energy and burns it away. This is a skill we could all use: to take the toxic energy in our lives and use it as fuel. In many ways, the Knight of Wands is talented in the arts of transmutation and alchemy. Though not as skilled as the Queen and King, the Knight is certainly no slouch at taking something dangerous and harmful and turning it into something productive and beneficial. Through your work with this Knight you will also learn how to keep your creative and spiritual spark burning, even when it feels like the world is doing its best to snuff your light out. I hope your clothes are flame resistant!

The Knight of Cups may be a bit of a romantic, but they know how to use one's heart to create a life worth living and loving. This Knight is all about the "feels," even if it ends up getting them into trouble or causing self-inflicted emotional pain. If this Knight can't feel it, then this Knight is not going to do it, end of story. Emotions are really tricky things, and I know I am guilty of sometimes wishing I never had any at all. It sure would make life easier if we didn't have to constantly wade through every single emotion we have—fear, doubt, regret, sorrow, grief, resentment, and anger. Life would be so much more fun if all of those things never existed. Unfortunately, emotions are an important part of the physical game. They are our navigation system and literally guide us from one phase of our lives to another, and the Knight of Cups is an excellent navigator. Sometimes this Knight is depicted with their eyes closed, showing how this Knight is able to tap into something other than physical sight to move and stay on top of the horse they ride. This Knight is well on the way to understanding how to use the power of one's emotions to benefit one's path. This meditative process of "feeling" your way through each moment is not easy to learn, for there is a lot of detachment involved. You see, it is one thing to attach to your emotions, but it is quite another to let them go and merely see how they influence, guide, or trigger your responses. As I said, emotions are tricky things. They can limit you or expand you. They can give you life-affirming energy or leave you feeling depleted and drained. Emotions can guide you toward the life of your dreams, or they can get you lost in a world of darkness and pain. Let this Knight guide you through the first steps of detachment. Let the Knight of Cups show you some of the tricks they have learned to stay focused and disciplined in the sea of choppy, emotional waters. Most of all, let this Knight heal and open your heart, so you can learn to love feeling again.

The Knight of Pentacles is a being of slow and steady movement. This Knight won't be rushed and believes that the only way to build a strong and lasting foundation is to lay it one brick at a time. That is exactly the way this Knight engages with all aspects of the physical realm: one piece at a time. The Knight of Pentacles is not one to multitask and considers this line of thinking and doing to be flawed and misguided. This Knight believes you should give yourself totally to the moment, to whatever task, person, problem, or situation you find before you. Anything less would be disrespectful. The slow, steady pace of the Knight of Pentacles is going to be hard for some people to deal with, especially considering we all seem to live in a world that moves faster than we have time to comprehend. It is not easy being a slow and steady person in a fast-paced environment. Sometimes it makes you a target, and other times it makes you invisible. Sometimes being both of these things can be beneficial. When people start to attack you for being too slow or taking too long, or accuse you of dragging your feet, just remember that your way of doing or being does not have to conform to anyone else's timeline. The Knight of Pentacles is very aware of this, and is used to being left behind by the other Knights, as they eagerly ride off for some form of adventure. Being left behind makes you feel invisible, but at least you no longer have to hear about how long you take getting things done. Training with the Knight of Pentacles guarantees that when you commit to something, you do so completely and fully, and make sure it is done in the right way in divine time.

PATHWORK

Intentional

Most of us tend to sharpen the skills we are already good at and put off things we don't usually excel in. Knights must sharpen all their skills, not just the ones they are good at. They have to practice and practice and practice. Part of that practice is meditation and visualization. This is such an effective part of skill-building that 90 percent of the world's top athletes also use this mindfulness technique to sharpen their skills. Now it's your turn. Pick a skill that you truly want to learn, even though right now you are just miserable at it. Maybe it's cooking healthy meals, maybe it's balancing your checkbook, maybe it's painting, maybe it's rock climbing. It really doesn't matter what it is; just be brave, pick your worst skill, and bring it to the meditation cushion along with a timer set for five minutes. Settle yourself by taking some nice deep breaths. Before you hit the timer and close your eyes, focus in on the skill you want to learn and see yourself doing it. Really get into the environment you see yourself in while using this skill—the people there, the clothes you are wearing, the expression on your face, and the feeling of your body. Tap into this, and then hit that timer, close your eyes, and stay focused on your image until your timer beeps at you. Repeat this as often as you feel you need to or until you start to see results.

Intuitive

Pull all four Knights out of your deck and place them facedown in front of you. Close your eyes, scan the cards, select the one you get an intuitive hit from, and turn it over. Whichever Knight you have selected is the one that you need to work with today, so go ahead and put the other three Knights back in your deck. Place your Knight either on your meditation altar or somewhere in front of you so you can keep your focus on the card. Relax into your breathing, drop your shoulders, and settle your mind. Keep your gaze on the card as you allow yourself to relax more deeply. Just keep your focus on the card in front of you and allow any thoughts, images, or chatter to just move on through your mind. When you feel focused and relaxed, go ahead and close your eyes. Stay still and silent for as long as you can, just letting the information or messages float in. When you feel done or no longer feel connected to the card and its messages, pick up your journal and write down any and all messages that this Knight sent you. Don't overthink this process by trying to question whether or not what you heard, felt, or saw was just your imagination. Just write it down; imagination or not, the information is important and relevant to where you are in this moment. You may want to do further journal work to go deeper with your Knight's message.

Wandering

For this exercise, you are going to have to either keep your smartphone with a note-taking app handy, or have a small journal and pen and carry it around with you for a whole day. Yes, this is going to be a whole day of mindful wandering, though it would be incredibly helpful if you kept it up for as long as you could tolerate it. Knights are meticulous about their habits, which is why they have a strict schedule and a fairly consistent routine. They know what they do with their time, how much energy they use on each task, and who they spend their time with. They also have gaps of time for relaxation, contemplation, and higher learning. Today you are going to wander through your day like a Knight, and you are going to track your life in the space of twenty-four hours. This is amazing mindfulness and habit training, as we typically just zombie our way through our daily lives. You want to be aware of everything you do from the time your feet touch the floor in the morning until you lay your head back on the pillow at night. Grab your phone or journal and begin your mindful wandering through a day in the life of you. Use the information you gather as a way to view how you use your time. Which habits suck your energy and which habits invigorate you? Let this data guide you to better manage your day and your energy.

QUEENS

You have now reached the stage of your development when it is time to bring your gifts, talents, and skills to a much bigger audience. No more practicing in the dark and only showing off to a few close friends. Think of this stage as being dragged out of the shadows of obscurity into the spotlight. Like it or not, none of us who has gotten to this level can escape attention from strangers. When we reach the position of Queen, we must understand that everything we have worked for and everything we have built has not been for us alone, and now it is time to give back. This is not always an easy thing to do, especially for us introverts, who, despite loving coaxing from all four of the Queens, will have to be dragged out from under the blanket fort we have built in the corner of our room. In many respects, the Queens are here to teach us how to take ownership of what we have created, and to stand proud and learn how to take a compliment, no matter how uncomfortable. The Queens show us how to take our rewards with grace and how to give back with a focused mind, an open heart, a generous pocket, and a true desire to help others.

The Queens have some of the most extensive networks in the tarot empire. There is nothing and no one these lovelies do not know, and connecting people is one of their favorite pastimes. This is another way you will know when you have entered into the stage of the Queen. You will know people, and not just any people, but people who can make things happen. You will be able to connect people to each other so that they too can advance along their soul paths. The Queens also have a lot of teaching energy around them, and they will impart knowledge, wisdom, and tricks of the trade willingly and without the need for coaxing or scheming. Just know that there will be some sort of payment involved, be it money, time, or whatever else the Queens deem necessary in exchange for the wisdom they share.

Does any of this sound familiar to you yet? Have you truly reached the level of Queen or are you just poking around? You may think you learned these skills while in training with the Knights, but the Knights' range of influence is small compared to the world that the Queens open up for you. Think about everything you have learned thus far and multiply it by fifty, because that is the growth that happens at this stage. You could say that it is in the court of Queens that you are finally stripped bare of all your foolish and childish ways and now dress in the regal robes of confidence, grace, power, and honor.

The Queen of Swords is no stranger to quiet, stillness, and alone time. One's best thinking is done in these simple moments, without distraction and constant interruption. This Queen knows the importance of space and is not at all afraid to let others know when they have had enough of people for the day. This Queen understands that the space inside their head is the most important space they have, and is very mindful of the thoughts, beliefs, and ideas that take up occupancy inside the mind. The Queen of Swords understands how easily you can allow limiting voices the opportunity to grab the mic in your brain. The Queen knows that if you are not vigilant, these scared, frightened parts of the ego mind can end up derailing you from the part you now play in the bigger, broader world around you. The Queen knows that you have not come this far or worked this hard to be so easily misled. Through meditation, the Queen will guide you on how to pluck these nagging doubts and inner critic voices from your mind to free up space for more empowering and life-fulfilling thoughts and ideas. This then allows people, places, and things to line up with ease and grace, as you have stilled the ego monster and paved the way for miracles to happen. The Queen of Swords learned back in training as a Knight that everything starts in the mind. Every hope, every dream, every doubt, and every fear—all seed in the mind. The more attention you give them the faster they sprout. In order for the Queen of Swords to rule, hold court, and be of service, they must constantly be weeding out anything that does not serve their higher calling. Pathwork with this Queen will teach you to do the same.

The Queen of Wands is like no other muse you will ever come across. This Queen is delightful, playful, desirable, and will literally set your world on fire. The Queen of Wands has gotten slightly better at standing still, though it is still their least preferred option. They have learned that sometimes even fire needs time to burn down and smolder for a while. Burning brightly all the time is exhausting, so this Queen has gotten more comfortable with kicking back and taking some downtime, as long as there is plenty of pleasure involved. Being pleasured is one of the Queen of Wands favorite pastimes, and they expect others to want to please them whenever and wherever they command. The ability to receive pleasure is not an easy skill to learn, as most of us are more eager to give than receive. This is why working with this particular Queen is so beneficial. I mean, what good is desire if you never allow it to bring you any pleasure? What is the point of all that manifesting, goal grabbing, and dream achieving if you don't take time to bask in its afterglow? At this stage in the game, the Queen of Wands has learned how beneficial it is to take a breath, or two or three, in between conquests. The Queen of Wands allows time in the day to truly marvel at what they have created. The Queen also spends time thinking about what others would like to create, for their creations will end up becoming part of the Queen's own experience. This is why this Queen wants others to use their creative talents wisely. You could say that at this phase of the journey, the Queen of Wands is learning to seek the pleasure found in the joy of others. The muse connects us all with an infectious and wildly spreading spark. There is no getting away from the creative energy that pumps through us all. It seems only right that we should allow it to bring us pleasure as well.

The Queen of Cups is not afraid to show their feelings. In fact, this Queen will wave them about like a badge of honor. The Queen of Cups doesn't care if you like this sort of emotional display or not, because this is how the Queen engages with the world and that is all there is to it. Flowing, intuitive, and heart-centered, the Queen of Cups doesn't have time for people who are too busy trying to mask, hide, and conceal who they truly are. The world is full of so many people pretending to be someone they are not and denying themselves feelings they are desperate to explore. But not this Queen. This Queen knows there is something liberating about throwing off all the masks and just being your authentic, messy, complicated self. The Queen of Cups knows how liberating it is to be fully engaged with people, places, and situations when you are not so busy trying to force your emotions to behave. When this Queen is feeling something, they show it. This does not make the Queen of Cups weak, or fickle, or even manic—quite the opposite. When people come to the Queen of Cups, they will always know what they are going to get. However, don't be fooled into thinking that this Queen wears a heart on their sleeve and does not have a brain between their ears. For the Queen of Cups sees you, all of you. They know what you think, how you feel, and how you respond under pressure. The Queen of Cups knows your strengths and your weaknesses and is not above exploiting both of them. A feeling Queen is a powerful Queen, and a powerful Queen is honored, loved, and, above all, respected. The Queen of Cups, like all the Queens in the tarot empire, has an expansive network and social circle. Pass the emotional tests this Queen has laid out for you and the Queen's world will open to you and grant you all your heart's desires. Fail the test and you could be locked out forever.

The Queen of Pentacles brings us back down to earth, oftentimes with a thud, especially if we have had our head in the clouds for longer than we should. This Queen is more of a doer than a dreamer and enjoys putting things together, tending to them as they grow, and gathering the fruits of long and constant hard work. This Queen prefers to be outdoors in the open air, as this is where their true magic lies: in the world of material things. Money and health are both equally important to this Queen, for they understand that one without the other is a futile and shortsighted pursuit. This is why this Queen will show you how to have a healthy relationship with both your body and your money, which makes the Queen of Pentacles a particularly helpful guide for the self-employed or the entrepreneur. Home based businesses are, of course, this Queen's speciality, for there is a true freedom to dictating your own hours, your own income streams, and your own way of creating the life that you wish to experience. A lot of times these things are overlooked in the pursuit of money, which is why the Queen of Pentacles brings us back to center, reminding us that money is useless when we have sick and suffering bodies.

The Queen of Pentacles wants to show you how to balance what you need with what you want. This Queen wants to show you how to create a life that is self-sustaining, beneficial to all, and, most importantly, secure and stable. Don't bother bringing your excuses to this Queen, because there will be no interest in what you have to say. The Queen of Pentacles will, however, be more than happy to show you how to create a life that you can enjoy, a life that you want to engage in each day, and a life that won't leave you with regrets or wondering "What if?" Just understand that all of this takes time, and the Queen of Pentacles is never in a hurry. You can't rush divine creation. It comes in its own time, in its own way, and on its own terms. But the Queen of Pentacles promises that when it does arrive, it will be more than you could ever have hoped and dreamed for.

PATHWORK

Intentional

Queens are networkers. They gather people, entertain people, and introduce people. They know who is who and what is what. They have a vested interest in all those they meet and are able to make recommendations and connections just by snapping their fingers. My mother used to tell me all the time: "It's not what you know, but who you know." A powerful Queen is not made overnight. They are strategic with their growth, and right now that is exactly what you need to be. Pick one of the four tarot Queens you wish to be or see yourself becoming, and start making the sort of connections this Queen would make. Act like your Queen would act, and move in the sort of circles you think your tarot Queen would move in. Perhaps your tarot Queen would throw a dinner party or even a fundraiser. Maybe the Queen you have selected would do charity work or seek out like-minded people through meet-ups and social events. Once you have decided on the Queen you want to be, sit with the card and allow yourself to visualize becoming that Queen—walking in that Queen's shoes; speaking the words you imagine they would speak; standing, sitting, and behaving the way you would expect your tarot Queen to. As you watch the scene play out, just be aware of anything in particular that stands out, as you may want to copy this later when your visualization is complete. Take as much time with your visualization as you feel you need. Do it as many times as you need to. And by all means, journal about how it feels to step into your tarot Queen's shoes. Keep in mind that you do not have to be an extrovert to excel at this. The online world is perfect for introverts, and it is just as capable of opening doors and connecting you with new and amazing people if you are intentional, joining online communities, courses, networks, and social groups. There is a tarot Queen for everyone. All you need to do is step into their shoes and place their crown on your head.

Intuitive

Do you ever think about your current circle of influence? This is the circle or collection of people that currently surround you and influence your decisions, whose opinions sway your actions, thoughts, and beliefs The Queens of the tarot know exactly how important this group of people is, for they have seen how kingdoms have risen and fallen based on the impact of those closest to their leaders.

For this exercise, you need one of the four tarot Queens, preferably the one that you feel is the closest personality match to yourself. Think about how you process and interact with people. Do you do it emotionally, intellectually, materially, or spiritually? One of these connects you to the one of the four Queens. Select one, and then place that Queen faceup in front of you. Now, let's take a look at the people or influences that surround your current Queen, as they will tell you a lot about what energy is molding your current vortex of manifestation.

Shuffle your deck and place one card above the Queen. This card represents the blessings in your current circle of influence. Now place another card below your queen. This is someone or something that is blocking you within your current circle of influence. Now place one card to your Queen's right. This card is for where your circle supports you. And lastly, place another card on her left. This is the card that shows the person in your circle who opposes your growth and success. You should have five cards in total—four cards surrounding your Queen of choice, who is in the middle of the cross-like spread. Turn them all over so every card is now faceup. Pull out your journal and start digging deeper through the influences you see around your Queen.

Wandering

In your life, you probably know the odd tarot Queen. Heck you might even know all four of them—your social circle may be made up of a mixture of all four tarot Queens. Being able to see the four Queens out in the world is a fabulous thing, because it makes it so much easier to find the one you need at the moment you need them. Which of your tarot Queens do you need right now? Which one has the connections, the list, and the contacts that will assist you in whatever task, goal, or project you are currently working on? If you can't find the four Queens in your social circle, expand your search, because I guarantee you have them in your world right now. Maybe it is someone you work with, someone who rides the bus with you, someone at your spiritual center, or even another parent at your kids' school. Somewhere in your life, the tarot Queens are playing their parts, just waiting to extend their knowledge and expertise to you. But you have to ask. You have to let them know this is something you want and need from them. Don't sit around waiting for the contacts you require or hoping the connections might just fall into your lap. You have to be proactive along this part of the path. You have to speak up, raise your voice, be clear and precise with your communication, and ask. The very worst that can happen is someone will say no, and that is not even a bad thing. It just means you have not asked the right Queen, or you have not asked the right question. Queens connect; it is what they are groomed to do. So keep moving through your world, seeking out the Queens, then ask, ask, and ask again.

KINGS

Welcome to the top of the pile, to the place where you will have to work harder then you ever have before, because now you are King and everyone wants your crown. It is true that there will be many who have no interest in being where you are once they see how much hard work and responsibility is involved, since they have no desire to work that hard. However, there will always be a handful of vultures just sitting and waiting to see how and when you will slip up, show signs of weakness, or falter on your path to self-mastery. For some, this stage is better than anything they could ever have imagined, as there are more amazing opportunities, more ways to show up and be of service, and even more ways to work with all the skills, habits, and gifts you have fostered in the last three stages. For others, the role of King will feel like a self-built prison from which there seems to be no escape. Not everyone is cut out to be King, but like it or not, this is where you are, so it's time to dig deep and look at all that you have learned.

Although it may seem like you have the choice to go back to life as you knew it, the reality is that you can't. You don't think the same way, you don't engage with your emotions and feelings the same way, you don't react or act the same way, and, above all, the material and physical world looks different to you now. You might be able to give back the crown, but you will never again be the person you used to be. You shed your skin back in the Knights. You were reborn and lovingly groomed with the Queens, and now you are a more aware, more aligned, more in-tune version of yourself. You are someone who is no longer capable of living life through the lens of all of those old fears, doubts, and limitations. This is the catch-22 of becoming King: you can't go back, even if you decide you don't want the crown, the glory, or even the fortune. You can only go deeper.

When you reflect on others who have reached this stage, what do you think about them? How you see people in places of power will influence how you work with the Kings during the pathwork exercises. Do you admire leaders in your field? Are you inspired by thought leaders and change agents in your community? Do you put famous people on a pedestal, or do you think their influence is all bullshit? Your answers will show where you hold bias toward power, leadership, expertise, and influence. Just remember, there is nothing wrong with having bias; we all have it in one form or another. There is, however, something wrong with hanging on to biases to our own detriment, for when you allow your biases to limit your experiences, you are the one who loses out.

The King of Swords has become a master of the mind. Thoughts, beliefs, and ideas are all carefully crafted and then released without an ounce of attachment. There is no plotting or scheming with this King. This allows for quick, flexible, and in the moment decision-making without doubt and anxiety. There is no need to be right when you can make *all* your decisions the right ones. There is no constant chatter in the mind that slows this King down or makes them second guess a course of action. This King has learned how to open up the mind and let it flow without the limitations of fear, regret, and anger. This allows the King of Swords to manifest quickly and easily, as if somehow everything just falls into place magically. The King of Swords practices meditation every chance they get, for a still, clear, calm mind really is this King's superpower. At this stage of the game, you will find that you will be able to make almost intuitive choices, as if you don't even have to think at all. You instinctively know what will work for you and what will not. You no longer waste your time on limiting ideas or mind traps that keep you from obtaining your goals, hopes, and dreams. As you engage in pathworking with this King, think about how, at this level, it is not about going further, but going deeper to find the stillness, the center, the core of your soul path. You have learned some amazing tricks to get you to the top of the hill, but how quickly you adapt and evolve will dictate how long you stay at the top.

The King of Wands can be volatile; there is no getting around it. When you play with fire for long enough, you start to wonder who and what it can burn the fastest. This King is forever needing to fuel their flames, which means they are always on the lookout for something to burn. Creative energy can be addicting and fire can only stay lit for so long. Unlike the other elements, fire is not something that can be maintained indefinitely, as it requires feeding. Constantly feeding a fire is hard and grueling work, and by now you have learned when to best harness and release this energy. You know when to stoke the flames and when to let the embers just burn in waiting. You have also learned that fire is an unpredictable energy and, as skilled as you are, you can't always guarantee safety and protection to those who come into your domain. At this point, people know to come to you at their own risk, which might make your time at the top feel a bit lonely. Even though people are drawn to your energy and flock to see you do your flaming parlor tricks, very few want to get too close to you. The King of Wands knows how to spot authenticity and integrity a mile away, and this also limits the amount of people who become part of this King's inner circle. As entertaining as the King of Wands is, nobody is quick to forget that they are also dangerous. Perhaps you like the thought of being dangerous, and this excites and thrills you. Deep down there may very well be a piece of you that craves the fear other people carry when they think of you. Or perhaps this bothers you and stops you from truly fulfilling your divine destiny, whatever that may be. This particular throne is only for those who can stand the heat, pardon the pun.

The King of Cups is no stranger to self-love, self-indulgence, and emotional mastery, with a helping of emotional manipulation on the side if necessary. This King has felt it all, as there is no feeling or emotion that they have not learned to control or work through. This King knows when emotions are weaknesses and when they are strengths. The King of Cups has played with and tested the limits of all those pesky human "feels." This King understands how to use the flow and ebb of their emotions to navigate and guide them along the path to success, health, and joy. There is an air of smugness about this King, and rightly so, as not everyone can get a grip on their feelings as quickly as this King does. Imagine being able to harness your most crippling feelings and use them to drive you forward. Think about what you could achieve if you knew that no matter what situation presented itself, you could handle it with ease and grace, never letting your emotions get the better of you. Perhaps then there would be more "yes" and less "no" in your life. What would that mean to you? The King of Cups is a "yes" person because they do not have to worry about what happens next, as they just deal with whatever rises and falls in the moment. There is real freedom to not being a slave to your emotions anymore. To finally be free of all of that draining energy is liberating. This is the level of life the King of Cups has achieved. This is the throne this King now sits upon, which is why this King can be prone to the odd bit of emotional manipulation, sometimes by choice and sometimes by accident, for they can't always be held responsible for the reactions or actions of others who have not yet reached the same level of mastery.

PATHWORK

Intentional

For this exercise, you need to find your inner King. The King that represents you at your best. The King that is in your zone—confident, driven, focused, and in complete control. Take the four Kings out of your deck and place them faceup in front of you. Which of these Kings best represents what it is you are trying to achieve? Do you own a business and want to be seen as an expert in your field? Do you want to be the King of your checkbook and master of your finances? Or do you wish to set the gold standard inside your family and be the inspiration you wished you had while you were growing up? There is a King for everyone once they know what they want to master, who they want to lead, and what influence they wish to have. So go ahead and pick your King. Select the card that is aligned to your personal aspirations, whatever they may be. Place this card somewhere you can see it throughout the day, perhaps on your altar, or maybe you need to take a picture of it and keep it as the lock screen on your phone. Whenever you catch a glimpse of your King during the day, repeat the following mantra: "I am King of my domain and I move through the world with confidence and ease." If you want to write a more specific mantra for your chosen King, go right ahead. But just remember, it should be quick, easy, and get you into the flow of the King's energy.

Intuitive

How do you envision the view from the top? Being King is not easy, nor is it often comfortable. But this is because most people never plan to be King. They don't really see themselves pulling it all off and mastering the mountain. This lack of planning often means your King status will be short-lived and possibly even traumatic.

In this exercise we are going to do a bit of forward planning. You are going to see this coming together, your moment of kingly glory, and embed it into your vibrational memory. Sit down in a comfy chair, take a couple of nice deep breaths, and start to imagine your perfect day. You have to imagine it from beginning to end, from the moment your feet hit the floor in the morning until you drop off to sleep at night. If you need to close your eyes to visualize this, by all means do so. If you can daydream with your eyes open, then do that. Make sure you soak up every detail, from the weather to what you are wearing to who you are sharing this day with. Allow yourself to really sink into this daydream. Listen to the conversations you might be having. Notice how your body feels, how your face looks, and how you are carrying yourself. Depending on how good of a daydreamer you are, spending about five to ten minutes will be more than enough for the visualization side of things.

Once you are done with the daydreaming, pick up your journal and write it all down. Title your page "My Perfect Day" and date it. This exercise takes the pressure off being King for a while, and instead reminds you why you want the things you do, and why you work so hard to both achieve them and keep them. Or maybe it shows why you climbed the mountain in the first place and why it is important to soak up the view for as long as possible. Before you know it, all of your Kings will be right side up and working to assist you in running and maintaining your personal empire.

Wandering

The Kings in the tarot can often represent a certain time of life or the senior part of our mortal journey. We enter this elder phase of our existence somewhere between sixty and sixty-five years of age. I work with many clients who are in their King phases of life, and they teach me so much about what it means to be an elder. For one thing, just because you made it to the King phase in your life hardly means you have everything figured out. Oftentimes, the longer you live, the more things you realize you don't understand at all. They also teach me the magic of time, and how with decades of time to view the soul's journey, they can pinpoint divine moments in their lives, seeing how the flow and rhythm of their lives has played out.

In this exercise, think about what you want to be doing in the King phase of your life. You might want to consider the following: What wisdom do you want to impart? What new skills or adventures would you like to have? What places would you like to see, and what do you want to do when you see them? Just relax into this exercise and let your mind wander into the age of the King, a place where age is revered, elders are respected, and your knowledge and wisdom opens new and exciting doors that before were hidden. Even if you are already in this phase of your life, hold the vision anyway. Allow your awareness to wander to places you have yet to travel to or to achievements you have yet to attain. Just breathe, relax, and wander through this King phase of your life, without rules, without restrictions, and, most of all, without judgment. If you wish, you can take your daydreaming to your journal and write this all up to explore it further.

4

· · · · · · · · · · ·

THE MINOR ARCANA

WELCOME TO THE REMAINING minor arcana cards, the Aces through Tens. You will notice that the intentional lessons for this chapter carry on from one number to the next, making the minor arcana look and feel like sequential steps that need to be walked along a specific path in order to get to a desired location. This is done on purpose, as most times the minor arcana cards are dealt with as if they are individual cards that are just hanging around waiting for the other cards in the spread to give them meaning and relevance. The truth is, these cards are already well-grounded into a story. They never show up alone, and they tease you with parts of a story that indicate both where you have been and where you are headed. The cards of the minor arcana suits are numbered for a reason, and to not work with these numbers and the steps they represent on purpose means you are missing out on such an important part of the tarot's teachings.

ACES

The Aces begin our journey through the four suits by introducing us to the possibilities each suit offers. I like to think of the Aces as dream seeds, full of potential with a story yet to be told. In this respect, the four Aces of the minor arcana are similar to the Fool card, for they don't really give you any indication of what is going to happen, only the prospect of something happening if all the conditions are aligned in the most divine way. The Fool is all about divine and inspired alignment and appears to trust that this is just how life is meant to be experienced. The Aces may not have the same sort of confidence the Fool has, but they do live in the field of divine potential where the Fool likes to wander. Unlike the Fool though, the Aces hint at the work that is to come, if you wish to go ahead and plant one of these dream seeds in your manifestation garden. The Aces will grow, but only if you care for them, nourish them, and do all the things that are required for them to fulfill their potential. We are each a dream seed, full of untapped potential and waiting for the right set of conditions to burst forth so we can be the best version of who we are and shine our divine light out into the world.

The Aces help us find out what sort of energy we need to focus on in each step of our physical journey. They represent something we are working on, be it a goal, a lesson, a relationship, or new skill. Each of the Aces offers us a different experience and a different level of engagement through which to see ourselves and the world around us. They show us what is possible without swaying us in one direction or the other. We get to choose how we will use each of the Aces by deciding if what is on offer is something we want or need. We also get to choose how much work we are willing to put into our dream seed, if we choose to plant it. Choices are key when working with the Aces, choices you get to make willingly most of the time. Sometimes when an Ace comes into our lives, it is more of a heads-up of what is to come, perhaps a new experience that is going to require you to put in some effort, whether you like it or not.

The Ace of Swords can get stuck in your head like an earworm, a constant looping song, mantra, idea, or conversation that just won't leave you alone, no matter how much you want it to. It can cause you to become single-minded and focused, or it can distract you to no end. As a writer, the Ace of Swords will often serve up wonderful ideas to me that become something marvelous, much like this very book you are reading. However, for the most part, it just bubbles up whatever seems to be floating around in the conscious mind at any given time. This is one of the lessons the Ace of Swords brings with it—discernment, which is knowing what to pay attention to and what to ignore. Get it right here and it won't cause you as much grief as you progress through the rest of the suit of swords. It is important to remember that not every idea that presents itself is one for you to take action on, as some are merely cerebral chatter. Learning how your mind works is the seed that is being offered up here. Take time with this Ace and get to know how your thoughts operate. Learn to distinguish between the constant chatter of the ever-processing mind and the vibration of inspired ideas that offer real potential. Seek out moments of quiet and stillness, so you can calm yourself and focus. Practice emptying your head through journal work or meditation so you can see what is left behind once all the noise has moved on by. Only then will you truly be able to see that gift that this Ace offers you.

The Ace of Wands is your personal magic wand. Even though all the Aces offer potential for growth, only the Ace of Wands offers you growth through magic. One of the issues many people have with the Ace of Wands is that it brings with it a lot of energy, and oftentimes it is restless energy that can be hard to direct and channel in appropriate ways. This can cause one to get totally and utterly distracted, or it can cause one to become paralyzed by feeling overwhelmed. This energy only grows and intensifies as we move deeper into the suit of wands, so take your time with the Ace and really learn how to use the magic that is being offered up here. The fiery nature of the wands makes them somewhat explosive in inexperienced hands, which means you might have a few mishaps along the way. But don't worry, it is all part of the learning curve. Once the thrill and excitement wears off, and it will, you can settle into exploring what untapped magic your wand offers. I should point out that this card offers something different to each person who works with it. Each magic wand is unique and merges in a unique way with whoever is wielding it. What you can create with your wand of potential is not what someone else can create with theirs. This is another lesson of the Ace, and that is to not compare your magic with someone else's. What is meant for you will come to you in due course, and what is not won't. It is as simple as that. Wands always work best when we have our feet firmly planted on the ground and open our hearts as wide as we dare. Only then will you see what sort of magic you are capable of creating.

The Ace of Cups is often depicted as overflowing and abundant. There is a piece of me that always wants to ask this card if it could please get a coaster and not spill all over my coffee table. This says a lot about how I see this card, as I don't like water all over the place and will do pretty much anything to avoid having to walk through puddles in my socks. I am sure there are those among you who love the idea of jumping in the many puddles this card leaves in its wake. But I like my water contained and controlled, which is why I always thank the sea for stopping at the shoreline and not washing us all away. I didn't realize I had issues with this card until I wrote the Animal Totem Tarot. The Ace of Cups was the very last card I wrote. It eluded me for weeks and was causing me great frustration. Eventually, through a lot of meditation, it finally dawned on me that I truly did not believe in the story this card was offering up, which was the never-ending universal supply of love, wealth, health, happiness, and joy. I was seeing this card through the lens of my personal lack, meaning I was totally disconnected from the card and its gifts. Of all the Aces, this one is the hardest to put into practice for most of us. Sure, we get the Ace of Cups in theory, but what about when it comes to the divine flow and abundance of our day-to-day lives? What do we think we are really worth, and how does that value show up in our experience? There is a lot of healing energy within this card, but in order for you to tap into it, you have to feel worthy of it.

The Ace of Pentacles seems like a gift from the heavens, but in reality it is all about being on the earth and seeing what's already here, in order to create something that may appear to be a miracle. If you compare the Ace of Pentacles in the Animal Totem Tarot with the Ace of Pentacles from the Llewellyn Tarot you will notice the difference in its representation. One shows the pentacle on the ground, being worked and moved, while the other seems to be miraculous in its giving, as a giant hand plucks a golden coin from the sky. I sometimes wonder how often the perceived nature of this card trips people up. The Ace of Pentacles, in my experience anyway, is the card of blessings. What you bless increases. The art of blessing starts with what you have and what you currently see, feel, touch, smell, and hear. This includes your body, which brings up an interesting question. How many times a day do you bless your body and give thanks to it for allowing you to experience this physical realm? The body is the true material gift, for without it, we would not be able to engage with anything this physical plane has to offer. Through the act of blessing, we tend to attract more of what we bless. Doing so will bring more work, more joy, more abundance, or more responsibility. This is the gift unseen, but it starts with its feet firmly on the ground and with what you already have.

PATHWORK

Intentional

One of the most fun ways to work with the Aces is to picture them as actual seeds, which is how I work the them most of the time. I am going to show you how to use the Aces on purpose, to either bring you something you want or open the door to an opportunity you really wish to experience. For this exercise, you need to pick just one of the Aces. Do you want to grow a money tree, a creative spark, a new relationship, or an idea? Once you have selected your Ace or seed, remove it from your deck and place it in a clear glass jar along with a clear quartz crystal (this is to magnify the energy of your path and spellwork), some salt (for protection, as it is important to protect your seeds), and a teaspoon of dirt or potting soil (as your seeds need something to grow in). I recommend you wrap your dirt and salt in some cling wrap and seal it before you put it in the jar, so you do not damage your tarot card, or photocopy your tarot card and put the paper replica in the jar instead of your actual card. Once you have all of your items in your jar, put the top on it, and place it either on your altar, the top of a bookcase, or anywhere else it won't be disturbed for the next seven days. You will also need some abundance incense and seven green candles, one for each day you are going to be doing this work.

Now that you have your jar, your incense, and your candles, you are ready to get to work. Remember, you are planting seeds, so you have to be able to see what it is you are growing. This is where your meditation or visualization is going to be important, which is why I recommend doing this ritual for seven days. That way it will hold your focus and amplify your manifestation power. If you have your jar, incense, and candles all set up on an altar, go ahead and get comfortable, as if you are about to meditate, chant, or pray. If you have your items on a shelf, bookcase, or bedside table, pull up a seat and get comfy. Go ahead and light your incense, placing it next to your sealed jar, then light your green candle and focus on the flame as you settle your breath and your body into the moment. When you feel relaxed and grounded, start visualizing your seed fully grown and manifested as a tree, idea, relationship, or creative project. Marvel in all of its amazing splendor. Take in the sensations and notice how happy, joyful, or full of pride and accomplishment you feel. Make this vision as big and as bold as you possibly can. Make it vibrate with color and sound to the point that you could reach out and touch it. Hold that image for as long as you can, and when you feel you are done, bring your hands to prayer position, bow your head slightly, and just say "Thank you." If you need to close your eyes for this, go ahead. Let the incense and candle burn all the way down. Cone incense and small altar candles usually take about thirty minutes to burn. Obviously, do not leave these items unattended. Repeat this for seven days. You will be amazed at what you will grow if you follow these simple steps.

Intuitive

Sometimes we don't know what seeds we want to plant or what seeds we should be planting. Oftentimes this confusion is brought about because our head wants to go one way and our heart wants to go another. The best method is to let your intuition choose for you. In order to do this, you will first need to remove your Aces from your deck. Put them facedown in front of you and shuffle them as they remain facedown. Then go ahead and select one. I sometimes like to choose the one that either has heat emanating from it or creates prickling sensations in my hand as I slowly scan the cards. If you draw this card upside down, turn it right side up.

So what did you pick? Is it what you thought you needed, or is it a match for what your heart has been crying out for? Either way, use this card, and do the same exercise we did in the intentional section, as I want you to grow the seed of your intuition. Trust that your intuition knows what it is talking about, and that it wants to align you to success in all of its forms.

Wandering

In this exercise see if you can find the four Aces throughout your day. Be on the lookout, raise your awareness, and move as if in a walking meditation. Be mindful of what people say and do. Pay closer attention to where you end up during the day. Read street signs and take in landmarks. You are on the lookout for four things:

1. A new opportunity to increase your abundance, be it money or health

2. A new possibility for a deeper emotional connection to someone or something

3. A new spark of creative potential

4. Last but not least, a new seed for an idea or a potential new class to expand your current knowledge

I am always surprised by where I find these sparks. I suggest you write each one down as you find them. Think of this like the once-popular game Pokémon Go, but for the four Aces of the tarot instead.

TWOS

With the Twos in your orbit, you know it is time to bring someone or something into your life to help you with your current goal, situation, or problem. The Twos teach us how to work and play with others. No matter how much we like to think we are alone in this world, we are not, and the Twos remind us that we all work in partnership with someone or something. Writers need publishers and readers, without which their writings would never be seen. Companies need innovators, marketers, and customers, otherwise they would never be able to create a product and have people buy it. No matter what you are doing in your life, I can guarantee you are in partnership with someone or something. If you have a job that provides a consistent paycheck, you are in partnership with the people who pay you for your time. If you freelance, you are in a partnership with your clients. I could go on, but I think you get the idea. When I work with the Twos in a magical sense, I use them to bring me the part of the puzzle which I myself may not be able to find. In other words, I actively seek out a partner through the Twos. It might be a person to share the experience with, it might be someone to keep me motivated and who inspires me to keep going, it might be choosing just one idea and firmly committing to it and giving it my all, or it could be seeking balance with all the blessings that the Ace of Pentacles has bestowed upon me. Either way I am very deliberate when working with the energy of the Twos, and I highly recommend you take the same approach. Therefore, only work with one of the Twos at a time, as you want to keep a single focus while dabbling in the realm of partnership and duality. In fact, the more singularly focused you can be, the better partner you will be, and, in turn, the better partner you will attract. So be specific, laser in, and keep your mind and heart aligned with one single intention.

The Two of Swords reminds us that we have to make a commitment to an idea. I know this sounds strange, but it is true. Many times, people never truly commit to an idea. They won't walk the path the idea opens up for them, and they are already dating other ideas the moment they start to get bored. This is one of the traits of unsuccessful people. They can never commit to an idea long enough to see any real results. The Two of Swords wants you to first make a decision and then, second, commit to it, give it your all, be faithful to it, and watch how it grows and evolves. Elizabeth Gilbert talks about this concept in her book, *Big Magic*, as it is a problem many creative people have. Don't get me wrong, not every idea is for you, and not every idea is going to bring rewards, but if you never give an idea a try, you will never know which is which. Therefore, just do it already. Make a decision and commit to it. See what doors it opens, or closes for that matter, and really walk the path with your decision. Published writers know that they often have to invest hours into an idea or concept before they know if it is going to lead to anything. We often call this the ten thousand-word test, for if you can get your idea to ten thousand words, there is a good chance you have an actual book in the making. If, however, you can't, then it is time to maybe reconsider your direction and see if retracing your steps might be helpful. For most of us, it takes time, effort, and energy to get those first ten thousand words written. We fully commit to the idea before we even know where it will end. This is one of the great lessons the Two of Swords has to teach us. Commitment equates to time, but not necessarily with the results you have in mind.

The Two of Wands brings a nice spark, a burst of growth and motivation to any situation. If in the Ace you had one magical wand, here you have two. Just be careful, as you want to make sure you are growing the right things and making headway only on the things your heart wants to achieve. This card can bring with it temptation, distraction and an illusion of power. This card has the energy of a young Mars testing his power under the watchful and loving gaze of Aries, which, let's face it, makes Mars more than a little cocky. When someone is too sure of themselves, they tend to make mistakes, get sloppy, and forget why they are doing something in the first place. It is easy to let the energy of this card distract you, but this card is put to much better use when it is supporting and empowering you. You want to approach this card with some humility; you will see better results if you do, even though there is a temptation here, with Mars at your side, to let the ego strut its stuff. Having two magical wands at your disposal can make you feel incredibly powerful, but it can also make you impulsive and reckless, so really think with your heart before you start waving these gifts around and aiming them willy-nilly.

The Two of Cups will bring you an ally in someone who shares your feelings, beliefs, and vision. I know a lot of people think this card is about lovers, and matched with the right cards, it can spell the initial spark of attraction to another in a romantic way. But generally speaking, this card is a nudge from the universe to invite someone else into your life to help with whatever issue, problem, or challenge you seem to be having. Think of this card as the "two heads are better than one" card. When this card pops up, you will know it is time to seek someone else's guidance, support, or advice. Your thinking related to some particular matter may have hit a wall, or you may be struggling to see a situation from another perspective, but when you find someone who shares your spark, who gets moved by the same things you get moved by, they offer up some brilliant and fascinating points of contemplation. We don't all see and feel things the same way, and because of this, we often never get the whole of anything. We only align to the bits and pieces with which we share a common bond. Other people also only see bits and pieces of the whole, which is why bringing someone else into the equation gives you more bits and pieces to ponder. Two heads really are better than one. Think about what areas in your life feel incomplete or where you feel like there is something you might be missing. Chances are the right person has been waiting in the wings this whole time for you to open up a space for them to come into your life and help you out.

The Two of Pentacles is a super active card. All of you needs to be engaged when this card dances or staggers into your life. If you blessed the hell out of your life in the Ace of Pentacles, then you have managed to double your blessings here in the Two of Pentacles. Congratulations! The only problem is now you have more to do. You have more demands on your time, energy, and body, which could have you literally juggling between that which needs to be done and that which you would like to be doing. That Ace really should come with a warning label. Oh wait, it does! It can be easy to get caught up in the never-ending action of this card. You may very well feel like you are always trying to manage your time, control your spending, focus on what you are eating, and rewrite your to-do list, but all of these things are just new to you. You are still learning to have a relationship with all of these new blessings. You haven't really negotiated the terms of engagement with any of them, though now might be a good time to consider doing just that. Let's face it, you can't juggle forever. Eventually you will get things under control and life will seem less hectic, but you have to start where you are. So use this time to take a good look around and observe this new landscape. What is really important to you now, and what will be important to you moving forward? What items do you need to be focused on, and which ones can you delegate? The Two of Pentacles ushers in a temporary state of busyness, but it is not one that is meant to last or set you up for failure. Instead, it is meant to push you to expand, grow, and tap into the things that are most life-affirming.

PATHWORK

Intentional

In the Aces, you planted a seed, one that you want to grow and see become your heart's desire. Here in the Twos, you start to learn that you never create anything on your own. You will need others to help you, guide you, support you, and possibly even heal you. There are four possible ways for this to happen, but just like back in the Aces, you can only pick one. So, sit with each of the Twos and really consider what your seed needs to help it grow. The Two of Wands will bring extra energy to your seed. It will enhance its magic, and if you have been having trouble focusing on your seed, it will give you a much-needed bout of inspiration. The Two of Wands will light up you and your seed, bringing energy and illumination to your dreams and goals. The Two of Swords offers you a choice between using your head and using your heart. The Two of Swords can't be used at the same time, but they can be interchanged, which means you have two superpowers at your disposal to help your seed grow. You will have the logic for weeding out the past and keeping your mind and imagination focused to see the seed fully grown. The Two of Pentacles will help you, if you feel you are juggling what needs to be done and what you want to get done. It will support your current balancing act, so you don't feel overwhelmed or exhausted. The Two of Cups will bring you someone who will believe in you and everything you are trying to achieve. This person will be emotionally invested in seeing your seed grow.

Based on this, which card is the right one for you? Do you need some extra inspiration, or a way to release the past while focusing on the future? Do you need some help with keeping up with all of life's demands, or do you require someone to share your vision and infuse it with love? Select the card that is right for you and place it in your spell jar, just like you did with the Ace, though this time, you want a rose quartz and some ground ginger to add to your jar. Write a small mantra, spell, or prayer for your card, based on what you have selected it for, and light a pink candle. Recite your mantra, spell, or prayer and spend at least ten minutes a day visualizing your Two working its magic on your seed. Do this for as many days as you feel necessary, then discard the contents of your jar and keep your energy-infused crystal with you for the next couple of weeks.

Intuitive

For this exercise, you are going to intuitively choose a personal assistant from the four Twos. In many respects, the card your intuition selects for you is the card that will best support, guide, and move you today. First, you are going to need to remove the four Twos from your deck. Place them facedown in front of you, spreading or fanning them out. Next, close your eyes and take some nice cleansing breaths, as you just focus on who would be best suited to be your assistant for the day. Place your hands over the top of the cards. You don't need to be touching them, but if it feels more natural to do so, go right ahead. Feel your way over the cards and select the one that either gives off some heat or some cold, or makes your fingers tingle. The energy of the cards feels different for everyone, so trust that whatever sensation you get from the cards is the right one for you. Now go ahead and turn your card over, and take a look at it. This is your guide for the day. Ask your card questions, use it as a point of reflection before you make a move, and think about how it can help you get through that to-do list with ease and grace. It may even give you a clue about who you should ask for help or who you could connect with to move a current project forward.

Wandering

For this exercise, as you walk through your day, you are going to find one of the Twos in your environment. Let's say you are at the park and you see someone walking two dogs who look like they want to go in two different directions, and the dog walker looks like they are struggling with juggling the two dogs. Hello Two of Pentacles! Perhaps you are walking along the sand watching the surf as it rolls in and out, and you see a flash of a fin, and notice two dolphins making their way across the waves. Hello Two of Cups! You could even be getting a morning coffee at Starbucks and find yourself with two hot, steaming cups of coffee. Hello Two of Wands! On your morning walk you might come across two paths and have to choose which one you will take. Guess who—yep, the Two of Swords. I think you are getting the idea. The idea is that the tarot cards will find us when we need them. Right now you need help from the Twos, so let them show up along your path today. Allow the card that wants to work with you to just materialize and see what opportunities show up with it.

THREES

As we progress through the minor arcana cards you will notice a bit of trend: we start inviting more people, places, and things into our lives. And the Threes just got very social. Under the Twos you learned about partnerships—how you work with one other person, thing, or situation at any given time. Here in the Threes we bring in as many people as possible for you to get done what you need to get done. Threes tend to be tactile in nature and are not at all afraid to let their hair down or wear their emotions on their sleeve. Each one of the Three cards of the minor arcana will share with you a different aspect of the Threes' personality, and you might notice just from looking at these cards in your deck that they do seem to go from one extreme to another. This is because there is no middle ground here in the world of the Threes. Balance is not something natural to these cards, yet they will try to create conditions for which they feel more balanced. Through these cards, your interaction with the world will broaden, and you will need to consider what your part in the larger picture of the world really is. In other words, what is the part you came to play, and how does that part join with the parts others around you are playing? This may lead you to question the intentions you set under the Aces. For the most part, you will learn that your goals, dreams, challenges, and blessings aren't as much yours as you think they are. You will start to see how your decisions impact others, and how the people, places, and things you encounter are interconnected in ways you never stopped to think about.

The Three of Swords is the most extreme of the all the Three cards, for where the others show the joy of engaging in the world and the people in it, this card shows isolation, pain, suffering, and grief. This card is often described as the heartbreak card, due to the nature of the Three of Swords shown sticking out of a heart, as you can see in the Llewellyn Tarot's depiction of this card. However, as I said in the opening paragraph, Threes can and do wear their hearts on their sleeves. They feel deeply, which means they are very sensitive to others' pain and suffering. They will often feel this pain as if it is their own, and can become indulgent in it, moving them out of empathy and into self-inflicted torment. There is a good chance this card is you carrying around pain that was never yours to begin with. The problem is that you have carried it for so long it feels like it belongs to you, and somewhere along the line you have taken ownership of it. This card is a reminder that others' pain is not for you to take and claim. By all means, show empathy and compassion, but don't cross the line where your ego turns you into a martyr. The suffering of others is just that, their personal suffering. It is part of a larger karmic cycle that has nothing to do with you. Your role here in the Three of Swords is to feel it, transmute it into compassion, and send it back into the world as love. Do not hold onto it and add even more suffering to the world. Remember: what you feed grows, so be careful when it comes to feeding more pain.

The Three of Wands wants you to get up close and personal with the world around you. This card wants you to immerse yourself in your manifestation process and engage with all of it. It wants you to dream big, visualize daily, take bold and decisive action, and expect miracles. This is the card that is often linked to the law of attraction. The Three of Wands is the polar opposite of the Three of Swords, for here we see hope and joy at the possibilities that the material world has to offer. Creation is celebrated in this card through the act of engaging in the process and allowing oneself to experience each step of the process as if it were an intimate lover. This is exactly how you should approach the art of manifestation. You should be able to see every detail, feel every curve, and walk around with a bit of knowing swagger in your step. Fire knows no fear or doubt. It only knows results, and here in the Three of Wands, we get to see just how well Mars taught you how to play with fire in the Two of Wands. As the energy and intensity of this card builds, the signs of your manifestation energy will grow, and before you know it there will be no doubt in your mind that what you are working to create is on its way. All you have to do is keep going deeper with your law of attraction process and make sure you are feeding your fire all the right ingredients to keep it burning.

The Three of Cups is the ultimate social card. This is the card about good friends, wonderful work colleagues, fascinating strangers, and fellow travelers. This is the card of weekly coffee get-togethers, dinner parties, work events, concerts in the park on warm summer evenings, and telling stories of shared experiences. No matter how you cut it, there is no "I" in this card. It is not alone, single, or left out. It is a part of something, inclusive and accepted for the part it plays. This card comes up a lot for me when it is time for me to reconnect with friends after having been an introverted hermit for far too long. It is a nudge from the universe to go out and play, laugh, enjoy the company of others, and allow myself to feel the love and support from other people in the world around me. Even the most introverted of us need some form of social interaction. We may not need as much as the extroverts of the world do, but we do need it, and the Three of Cups is a reminder that this is an important part of your physical experience. It is a crucial element to our journey here in the material world. To ignore this part of who we are, or to make excuses as to why we cannot be out in the world having fun, is to deny a huge part of the creation and manifestation process. Remember, there is only so much you can do alone. You need other people to help bring about your dreams, your goals, and your desires. There will always be a need for interaction and engagement, and avoiding it will only cause you frustration, anger, and suffering.

The Three of Pentacles is one of my favorite cards, as it shows what can happen when we all bring our talents and gifts to the table. This is the card of collaboration, or, more to the point, success through collaboration. This is the card that says, "You do you, I'll do me, and together we can work, live, and love in harmony." Each of us has a gift—yes, even you—and we have this particular gift for a reason. Your gift is for you and you alone. No one else on the planet does what you can do in the way that you can do it. It is what makes you so darn special. When you use your gift in conjunction with other people's gifts, amazing and miraculous things can happen. This card reminds me a lot of what it is like to create a tarot deck. There is the deck creator, the artist, and the publisher. Each one has a very specific role to play in the process of creating a tarot deck and getting it out into the world. The deck creator comes up with an idea and literally builds a complete vision around how the deck will look, feel, and be interacted with. This is then given to the artist, who brings this idea to life in a very visual way. The publisher guides this process with another amazing team of project managers, art directors, editors, designers, salespeople, distributors, and many other incredible team players. Each one of these people brings their gift to the project, and they only play that particular part. By using their unique gift and playing the part that is true for them, they create amazingly beautiful products that are shipped out to people all over the world. This is collaboration in action. It is beautiful and fulfilling, and creates amazing, miraculous things. People make other people's dreams come true, and there is just no avoiding it.

PATHWORK

Intentional

The Threes have a lot to teach us about how to create a team and how to work well with a team. In order for your seed to grow into the magnificent thing you want it to be, you are going to need to gather a team to assist you. Each of the Threes offers a different approach to team building, so let's see which one suits you and your needs the best. The Three of Pentacles brings people into your project, people with the gifts and skills you need but do not have. The Three of Swords is what Sonia Choquette calls the "Team of Seeing Eyes." This is when other people hold your vision right along with you. They never let you waiver or fall, and they constantly prop you and your goals up, like your own personal cheerleading squad. The Three of Wands brings action and action-oriented people with it. These are people who can help you promote your dream seed or who can connect you with other people who might be interested in your dream seed and want to actively help you anyway they can, so you can be free to keep your creative fires burning brightly. The Three of Cups is the heart-based team, which is the team of peeps that are just as emotionally invested in the success of your dream seed as you are. They want to be there for you to ride the highs and the lows, to give their time and energy, and to make you and your seed feel as loved and nurtured as possible. I am a big fan of the Three of Cups team.

What type of team do you need for your current dream seed? Remember, you only get to pick one. This will be the team you will work with to keep your dream seed alive and to feed it as it grows. Once you have your team selected, grab the corresponding card out of your deck and put it on your desk or beside your bed. This one does not go in a spell jar, as this card is magic all on its own. You want to see this card as many times as possible during the day, since you will want to constantly connect with it and make sure you are really focused on creating the correct support for the dream seed you planted back in the Aces. Every time you see your card, stop whatever you are doing and repeat the following mantra: "I have an amazing team working alongside me to make my dream seed grow and bloom. I am truly grateful for all the love and support." That's it! Do this for as long as feels necessary and just watch as your team pulls together to move energy faster than you ever could alone.

Intuitive

The Threes in the minor arcana are connected to the Empress card in the major arcana. You could say within each of these cards is an important message from the Empress herself. It is a message of something she wishes you to reflect upon and possibly even heal from. In order for you to see which message the Empress has for you, go ahead and remove the four Threes out of your deck and place them facedown on a flat surface in front of you, making sure they are all lined up the right way. Take a few deep grounding breaths and ask the Empress what it is she feels you need to be working on or with right now. Scan the palm of your hand over the cards until you feel some sort of sensation in your hands or fingertips. Go ahead and select one card, then turn it over so you can see it. Turn the card upside down. Look at this card from a totally different angle, see it in a way you have not seen it before, and use it as your point of reflection and the basis of your meditation for the next few days. Our guides don't always talk to us in direct or logical ways, which is why learning how to work with reversed cards, especially when we are asking for a direct message, helps us become more in tune with the subtle nature of vibrational communication. So, pick your card, turn it upside down, and open your journal—the Empress wants to talk to you through the energy of this particular Three card.

Wandering

The Threes are the trinity of the deck, even though there are actually four of them, which is weird when you think about it. But then again, there are no limits to how trinities or the power of three can show up in your life. For this exercise, I want you to become aware of how the power of three is playing out in your life. Let me give you some examples. I often write in threes, be it three twenty-minute writing blocks, or three sixty-minute writing blocks (Three of Wands trinity). I also tend to read in threes. I often have an audiobook, a book on my Kindle Paperwhite, and a book on my Kindle Fire all being read in the same time frame (Three of Swords trinity). I also have a trinity morning routine, which includes coffee, walk, and morning pages (Three of Pentacles trinity). In fact, the more I stop and think about it, the more I notice just how much the power of three affects my daily habits.

Now it's your turn. You are going to have to raise your awareness a bit for this, but as you make your way through your day, notice when a trinity is at work. Make a note of it and move on. Before you know it, you will be able to tap into your tarot trinity anytime you want or need it to assist you, support you, or guide you.

FOURS

If the Threes were about building a team, finding new friends, and learning how to work a room, then the Fours are about pulling everything you have learned thus far together, so you can build, grow, and become the person you set the intention to be when you were under the influence of the Ace. The Fours remind you that the person who has achieved all that they wanted to, including having the relationships, joy, and health they desired, is not the same person that started in the Aces. The Fours, in many respects, lay the foundation for the change that will come under the influence of the Fives, but for now it is about getting that foundation right and making sure you have all the things you require to keep expanding and rewriting all of those to-do lists and maybe even your initial intention. You want to check your initial intention and make sure it is still what you wish to create. Perhaps now that you have learned a few lessons, you want to refine your intention and make it even more specific than it was before. Here, under the very analytical eye of the Fours, you have to take a breath, have a good look around, and make sure everything is going according to plan. The Fours of the minor arcana suits have hints of the building energy from the Emperor in the major arcana. When in doubt, ask yourself, "What would the Emperor do? How would the Emperor proceed with this challenge or honor this blessing? Would the Emperor be happy with the results that are now showing themselves?" Remember, this is all about building to something you asked for back in the Aces.

The Four of Swords appears to many to be a bit of a passive card. I mean, how much can a person get done if they are asleep on the job? But in my opinion, sometimes you can achieve more by not doing than you can by doing. Sometimes it is best to separate yourself from what is going on and take a break, or as we say in Australia, take a mental health day. This card really wants you to rest your mind, to stop the internal chatter, to relax, and to unwind for a bit. Not everything can be solved in our heads, and not all things need our direct involvement. Remember how back in the Threes you learned about playing just your unique part in the world? Well, this time you and your gifts are being told to take the day off, and that the rest of your team has it. Letting go and disconnecting the mind is not as easy as it sounds, and for the most part, many of us fail at this. This is why you may see this card a lot if you are one of those people who struggles with detachment and has some control freak issues. There is a huge element of trust in this card, and your trust issues will be triggered under the reflective gaze of those four swords. Just remember this is all a good thing. It is a positive sign that you are being triggered, as it means you are being alerted to things that need to be healed, cleared, and meditated on.

The Four of Wands, more than the other Fours, has a real feel of structure to it. In both the Llewellyn Classic Tarot and Animal Totem Tarot, we see a physical structure—something that has been built or erected, and offers shelter or support to those around it. The Four of Wands can represent the four pillars of a joyful, balanced life, which includes health, abundance, family, and spirit. However, you can name your pillars anything you want. Everyone is building something different, so do not feel limited or stuck with any of the labels myself or others provide. Each of these wands is somehow magically still growing and blooming, which means each of them has the potential for more. What that more will be very much depends on what elements you use to build your foundation. There is an air of joy, celebration, and expectation in this card that can be infectious. The idea of the well-rounded, balanced, happy home life is a delicious vision, but I caution you from believing that it is suited to everyone. Not everyone wants to play happy family, and not everyone wants to settle down and stay rooted to the spot. Some could argue that this is a limited view of the Four of Wands, but for some, what is on offer here may not be overly appealing. This is why it is best to focus on the structure and what is being built that needs to be supported by that structure. Even if you are

THE MINOR ARCANA   151

a risk-taking, self-proclaimed singleton with no attachments, you will still need an element of structure and support in your life. The Four of Wands offers that to all without exception.

The Four of Cups is often referred to as the hangover card, mainly because it comes after the social gathering of the Three of Cups. Sometimes this card shows up as a lesson in overindulgence, but not always. This card plays with me all the time, and it is the card that lets me know that I have some work to do. I would rather do anything besides what is staring me in the face. Yes, giant cup floating in space, I'm talking to you. Sure, you offer me all of my hopes and dreams, but look, SQUIRREL!!! Doing the work to reach your goals gets boring real fast, and once all the lovely, shiny inspiration wears off, you hit the hard ground of reality with an unceremonious thud. When the muse has had her way with you, it can be hard to find that spark again, but the work still needs to be done. Like it or not, you are going to have to learn to move past the boredom and overwhelm, push through the excuses, and reach up and grab that damn cup. You may drag your feet, you may grumble, and you may even have a headache from the night before, but what other choice do you have? No one else is going to do your work for you, no matter how much you want them to, and I know you want them to. It would be so much easier to ... but did I mention, squirrel!

The lesson of the Four of Cups is not an easy one. It is hard to set healthy, empowering habits, and even harder to stick to them. But if you are to continue moving forward, if you want to keep growing, you are going to have to find a way to make friends with this card. If ever there was a card that can be one of your greatest allies, it is the Four of Cups.

The Four of Pentacles says, "Did someone mention a squirrel?" Don't look now, but there is that pesky but adorable squirrel right there on the Four of Pentacles in the Animal Totem Tarot. I think she is stalking you. Now don't get paranoid, even though that can be one of the energies of this card. Just chill and let our furry friend share its pentacle medicine with you. The Four of Pentacles is about learning the flow of the material world. What goes out must also come in, and vice versa. Things grow faster and stronger when they are flowing and unrestricted. But this sort of flow requires a certain amount of awareness and a firm hand. It can be the combination of these two elements that trips people up. They either get the awareness part and become a little too obsessed with what they do or do not have, or they master the firm hand and hold onto everything with a tight and closed fist. This card has a tendency to bring out the loudest fears surrounding your current state of abundance. Know that your current income level has nothing to do with it. I have seen millionaires be crippled by their money, and I have seen those with so little step into the flow of giving and receiving as if it were as natural as breathing. The trick with this card is to know what you fear, face it, and then grow anyway. Are you afraid of being homeless or running out of food? Do you not give to others because you are always worried about that rainy day that never comes, or do you give too much and leave yourself with nothing? The Four of Pentacles wants you to find your trigger, get up close and personal with it, and then do what the squirrel does, which is bury it so it can grow into something useful, supportive, and more giving.

PATHWORK

Intentional

Your dream seed is getting ready to burst forth, and if you have not laid the groundwork for its growth, how will you direct it? Your seed is going to grow one way or the other, so best to make sure you know exactly where it's going. Working with the Fours on purpose and with intention will help you ground your seedling and allow you to direct its natural flow. Don't be fooled by the lack of action in each of these cards, because there is a lot going on. In many ways, the Fours teach you what your part is in this crucial phase of the growth cycle. Do you need to go sit down, so that you don't corrupt the manifestation energy? Do you need to be more discerning with your resources and make sure you have enough to cover your next point of expansion? Is it time to give your team a much-needed boost by showing them how much you appreciate their love and support? Do you seriously need to get over yourself and get your head back in the game? Yeah, Four of Cups, I'm looking at you! Just like in the previous section, you can only pick one of the Fours for this exercise. Remember, you are picking this Four on purpose, full of intent. There are no mistakes here, so trust that you know exactly what the next step is and then decide it. Place this card on your altar or wherever you meditate or pray. When you sit down and do your daily mediation or prayer practice, light a candle and take a minute or two to connect with your card. Find a prayer or even a quote that works well with what you are trying to achieve with this card. Do this until you can feel the structure and support build up around you and your dream seed.

Intuitive

Sometimes we need the power of all four cards to really amp up our empire building skills. Remember, these cards connect us back to the Emperor. Each one of these cards plays a crucial part in the growing cycle of anything and everything we are working on or working toward. This is why this meditation is a great way to use the full power that the four elemental cards have to offer you. You can do this meditation with your eyes open as you read through the script; record it and play it while you close your eyes; or light a candle and lean into the journey. There is no wrong or right way to approach this; just do what feels comfortable to you.

Take a few nice deep breaths and just allow yourself to relax into the moment. Focus only on your breath as you release your attachment to the past and the future. Your breath is here, now, in this space at this time. You cannot take a breath from the past and you cannot take a breath from the future. All you have is right here, right now. Allow the energy of the Four of Swords to wash over you, relaxing your mind and your body as you stay focused and connected to this present moment. See these four swords cutting any and all distractions from your mind. Harness the energy of the Four of Cups as you keep yourself seated and focused on the work that is staying present in this moment, even if you feel like you would rather be doing something else. Feel the breath coming in through your mouth, hitting the back of your throat, and filling up your lungs. Let the demands of the outside world go as you sink deeper into the space that the Four of Wands has created for you. Feel yourself being supported and protected as you sink even deeper into your breathing, knowing that the Fours of the minor arcana are holding this space for you. As you keep your focus on the breath, use the energy of the Four of Pentacles to focus the breath even more. On each inhale, give thanks; on each exhale, send out love and compassion. Your physical body is a gift, an asset, and something that when blessed will only prosper more in its well-being. Blessing the breath and giving thanks to the breath allows you to support and appreciate all that you have, right now, at this moment. Take another deep breath, focusing only on the gifts of your current experience. The gift of space, the gift of health, the gift of focus, and the gift of support. Bless each of these as you give thanks to the Fours and release this meditative connection.

Wandering

In numerology, the number four is the glue that keeps all the other numbers together. It is not the most glamorous of numbers, nor the most exciting, but without it, nothing would ever get done. The four deals with things the rest of us would rather not know about. It is not flashy, but a quiet, gentle, miracle worker. As you make your way through your day, make sure you don't skip over the things that you consider boring. We all have to do things we don't enjoy in order to get to the things we do enjoy; it is just how all of this works. You can't build a house by starting with the roof. There are things in your life that you need to deal with, including boring, unexciting yet necessary things. So, take a nice deep breath, roll your shoulders out, keep your back straight and your chin up, and lean into the deeply grounding nature of the Fours of the minor arcana. Get done that which doesn't excite you, so that which does excite you can come out to play. If you need extra inspiration, remove the Fours from your deck and put them somewhere you can see them throughout the day. Let them be a visual reminder that necessary is the new sexy.

FIVES

Whether you like change or not, it is and will always be the only constant we have here in the physical world. There is nothing in our lives or in our knowledge—albeit limited—of the universe that escapes the inevitability of change. Nothing stays the same, ever. Yet despite this one constant, I am always surprised by how many people just can't get comfortable with change. They cling to the world as they think they know it, and hold on for dear life. Is it any wonder that so few people actually rejoice when they see the Fives show up in a reading? Your personal bias or beliefs about change will direct your response when one of these cards walks into your reading. The Fives in the minor arcana show all sides of our responses to change, from pain to loneliness to conflict, as well as what happens when you get into the vibrational vortex of change. These cards move us through all aspects of the energy that change brings into our lives. The Fives show us what things need to get left behind, and that some changes are meant to be made alone. The Fives also show us how to walk the path of change as a way to benefit ourselves and those around us. However, like most messages from our guides, these lessons can only benefit us if we are willing to hear them and allow them into our right now experience. As you learn to walk the vibrational path of the Fives, hopefully you will start to see them as indicators of growth and expansion and not harbingers of destruction.

The Five of Swords is often said to show victory at a cost, or, you could say, defeat at the hands of a self-important bully. It really does depend on how you view that "go get 'em" attitude. Not everyone is comfortable with the thought of winning at whatever cost, yet you probably hear people say they will do whatever it takes to make their dreams come true. Here in the Five of Swords that statement of doing "whatever it takes" is being put to the test. This card really does ask the question, "What are you willing to do for a small win?" When you decide to walk with this card, you will have to decide if you see winning as an act of personal growth or something that takes from someone else. You will also have to decide how you feel about your reputation. Wayne Dyer once said that when he would give a speech to one thousand people, one thousand different versions of his reputation would walk out of the door. In other words, what other people think or say about us is literally out of our control. What's more important to you as you walk around collecting all of those fallen swords? Is it what the people who walk away think of you? Or is it what *you* think of all you have achieved?

Remember, on your way to your dreams, there will always be those who want nothing more than to tear you down and see you fail. The Five of Swords asks you if you will let those people inside your head rent-free and allow them to dictate the terms of how you see yourself and the life you are working so hard to build. Never lose sight of the fact that the suit of swords represents thoughts and words that you repeatedly think, hear, or speak. These words are the Five of Swords you see on this card. They can all do harm, or they can all act as cord cutters, liberating you from the bonds of the past self, but again, it all comes down to how you decided to walk with this card.

The Five of Wands is a card I love to see in a reading. For me it is right up there with the Tower card. Funny enough, my personal reader always seems cautious to gauge my reaction when this card shows up. This is because most people see this card as a conflict, which of course it can be, but the thing I love about all the Fives is that none of them are set in stone. I see the Five of Wands as a challenge card, one that lets me know that I literally have five magical wands at my disposal, but it is up to me to get them organized and focus that energy onto the target of my goal. The energy of the wands is not a gentle energy to work with, so it really is easier said than done to get all of this energy to point in the same direction at the same time. This is why, for a lot of people, this card means conflict, possible aggression, and regret; but it doesn't have to be that way. Pathworking with the Five of Wands teaches you that when the challenge of fast-paced change shows up at your door, you don't have to continually hold your breath waiting for something to drop from the sky and crush you. I have no intention of sugarcoating this, as the Five of Wands is a difficult card to work with. But remember that as you get into the vibration of this card, the path does become a little easier, and before you know it you will be more than willing to hold those five wands in your hands and use them for what they were intended for: magic.

The Five of Cups in many ways illustrates the emotional consequences of change, what we get to keep, and what needs to stay behind. It indicates what emotions serve us moving forward and what emotions we have grown out of. In this respect, the Five of Cups is an indicator of emotional growth. The pain of loss and death of the old self are apparent in most versions of the Rider-Waite inspired decks. The feeling of sadness in this card is important. This is the emotion you need to feel, and to tap into, in order to have that burst of emotional growth necessary for you to be the version of yourself that you need to be to reach your goals, manifest your dreams, and grow your dream seed. One of the reasons many people turn to meditation is to better understand and control their emotions. Meditation allows you to see your emotions as something essential to your spiritual growth, but not important enough to dictate the terms of it. In other words, we learn how to use our emotions as a guide, but we never let them make our decisions. Pathwork with the Five of Cups is similar to this process. Think of the water as a flowing river upon which you are riding; as the river moves you along, the view will change, as will the people, places, and experiences. The experiences available to you farther down the river that you cannot currently see will be very different than the ones you are having now, but in order to have them you have to accept that your view is going to change. Allow yourself to feel whatever emotions arise as you leave the shore and embark farther down the river. However, don't linger there, or you will block the excitement and curiosity that the adventure is bringing your way. Think of the two upright cups in the card itself. The knocked down cups are the experiences you are leaving behind at the shoreline, and the upright ones are yet to be filled with what comes next.

The Five of Pentacles may not look like it is the card of comedy, with its cold wintery scene and forgotten and forlorn figures, but every time this card manifests itself physically in my life, it does so in such a humorous way. I don't know if it is because I have walked the path of this card so many times now when it shows up it seems like an old friend letting me know I may have my manifestation energy pointed the wrong way. Many interpretations of this card from the Rider-Waite school depict a truly miserable scene, but is the Five of Pentacles actually a miserable card? This is where pathwork can allow you to see that misery is really a matter of perspective. Sure, you might think that your car breaking down on the hottest day on record, when your mechanic is on holiday and you have no money in the bank because it's still five days until payday, is a miserable way to spend a day. You also may think that having the airline lose your luggage and the bank put a freeze on your debit or credit card due to suspicious activity when you only have $40 worth of cash with you for a four-day conference sounds pretty miserable also, but do those events actually cause misery? One could argue that these types of situations push us way out of our comfort zone, build character, and make us think about what other resources we have at our disposal. Like all the Fives, the more you walk with them, the more you see they are all pushing you to the same place, which is change. Doors close and challenges happen for a reason, and oftentimes we need to dig deep and prove to no one but ourselves that we can achieve our dreams, regardless of what obstacles line up before us. Just keep in mind that no one ever said birthing your dream into the world would be easy or pain free. Loss and change go hand in hand. So go ahead and grab that hand, and let it lead you to a place where new things are just waiting for you to show up and introduce yourself.

PATHWORK

Intentional

One of the best ways to get over the icky feeling most people get when they see the Fives in a reading is to intentionally work with them for as long as you feel pulled to do so. You will bring their energy into your day deliberately. No, this is not a lesson in masochism, but it is about getting you comfortable with being uncomfortable. This is also exactly how you are going to pick your card—choosing the one that makes you feel the most uncomfortable. When you look at the four Fives in a row, which one makes you feel the most hesitant? If you could avoid this card, why would that be? The reason you don't want anything to do with it means you really need to work with it.

Take a nice deep breath and lean into your unease. Slowly sink into the valley of the uncomfortable shoe and start talking out loud about all of the things you don't like about this one particular card. Get it all out, everything about it, how it makes you feel, and why you don't want to feel that way. Keep going until you have nothing else to say. Once you have finished your verbal exercise, stop and think about what change in your life is making you feel this way. All of the feelings and thoughts you just voiced more than likely echo how you feel about the changes now presenting themselves in your current situation. Continue this exercise until you start to feel bored with this card. Once boredom sets in you know you will have shifted your resistance to it and the change it will bring along with it.

Intuitive

Many times in my coaching practice I hear clients talk about knowing they need to make changes in their lives, but they don't know where to start, or they need things to change, but they don't know what needs to change. This is when working with the Fives can be incredibly helpful. For this exercise, pull the four Fives from your deck and place them facedown, one on top of the other, in front of you. Read this exercise through completely before you begin. Place both of your hands on top of your four-card stack, and close your eyes as you take three nice deep breaths. Keeping your eyes closed, spread the cards out and pick just one. Open your eyes and place the three remaining cards back in your deck. Either hold your selected card in your hand or place it somewhere you can easily gaze at it. Think about how you could fix this card. What solutions could you offer the figures in the card? Consider which figure on the card seems the most approachable to you and direct your solutions to that figure. Maybe you could even suggest to this figure how you see the scene in this card as an opportunity rather than a challenge. This exercise puts you into the position of the observer. Learning how to see challenging situations from an observer perspective allows you to view the change for what it is—normal, natural, and needed. Perhaps by talking to the figure in the card, you opened up some insights that you too will find helpful and that will move you out of a stuck energy and into a flowing one.

Wandering

If you are one of those people who doesn't like change, then working with these cards either deliberately or when they show up in a spread is going to be difficult for you. In fact, you would rather think of anything else than what these cards are saying. Well, guess what? I am giving you permission to do just that. For this exercise, you are going to need a timer of some sort. I want you to set it for two minutes, and then hit the start button when you are ready to start this exercise. Ready, set, go!

What is the first thing that pops into your mind when you look at the four cards of the Fives? Where does your mind take you? Follow your thoughts until the buzzer on the timer goes off. I encourage you to document this in your journal or somewhere you can locate it again. Where you allow your thoughts to go may be the answer for why you can never reach that one goal you have always wanted to achieve, why you can't ever seem to land the job you really want, or why you can't seem to keep a relationship for an extended period of time. The more you take notice of your ever-wandering mind, the clearer the path of escapism will become. And before you know it, you will be able to catch yourself before you get too far down the trail.

SIXES

After passing through the changes and challenges of the Fives, the Sixes are a welcoming sight. Although they may not offer you rest just yet, they do open up space for you to make clearer decisions about where you are headed and what sort of conditions hold the space for the next phases of your journey. The Sixes may not be what you expect, but they are exactly what you need, especially having just come through the energy of the Fives. In some ways, the Sixes are a bit like Temperance, as they offer you somewhere to gather your thoughts, look at your actions, consider the lessons and loves of the past, and prepare for your next point of expansion. Just like with Temperance, you cannot linger in the space they provide, even though it might be tempting to do so. The Sixes can be nurturing and nourishing, but at the same time they will require some work on your behalf. There is an element of personal responsibility in these cards that is impossible to escape. Perhaps you have been blessed up until now, and it is your turn to bless those who now need your assistance. Maybe what you have been through in the last five cards has you longing for the days before you ever started this journey. Possibly you have decided that, all things considered, you have done pretty well, you have had a few small victories, and now you are considering trying your luck somewhere new, where you have never been before. Decisions will need to be made, but not just yet. Allow yourself time to soak up the lessons the Sixes have to offer, as you will need them moving forward, regardless of what you decide. It may even be in your best interest to make your way around all four Sixes and experience what each of them has to give.

The Six of Swords is the card of journeys, but where that journey leads will depend on what changes happened under the Fives. For a mental card, there is a lot of movement here. You could be taking a journey of the mind and shifting your ideas and beliefs. You could be firming up mindsets and building better boundaries around new and exciting thoughts and sparks of inspiration. Or you could find yourself on a physical journey, literally moving from one place to another. There is no doubt that movement is happening. One of the things I have always found interesting about this card, and all of the many ways it has been represented from one deck to the next, is that we cannot see the destination of this card. Never have I seen a card that shows where we will end up once we have finished with the Six of Swords. Maybe this card doesn't know. Perhaps we ourselves are not meant to know. Instead, we are left with one single focus, and that is the journey itself. Far too often, we focus on the event of see-ing everything come together and we forget that we have to put one foot in front of the other in order to get there. It is a gradual process

of getting from where we started to where our dreams are fully manifested. We grow, change, and evolve over the course of that journey,
often becoming new and different versions of ourselves. So where
are you now? Who are you now? How much further do you have to
go before you are the person who can live the life you want to live?
The Six of Swords is here to help, guide, and support you to go from
one version of yourself to the other.

The Six of Wands wants to congratulate you on a small but significant victory. It is probably just excited you made it through the
Five of Wands in one piece. Not blowing yourself or others up is
always something to celebrate. You might not see it as much of
an achievement, but it has far-reaching repercussions. One of the
lessons I have learned while working with this card is that small victories are far more important than the larger ones, for if we didn't
get the small wins, the big ones would never happen. That is why I
tend to see the Six of Wands as the personal win card. It's like when
you accomplish something small in your day that would normally
go unnoticed or unappreciated. It could be things like cleaning out
your closet and throwing away all the clothes that have holes in
them and donating everything else that no longer fits or interests
you, or decluttering your garage so your car can finally fit in it. It
could even be treating yourself to something special, just because
you bloody well deserve it! The Six of Wands teaches us to never see
any accomplishment as unworthy. Size is irrelevant with this card,
and titles like "big" and "small" have no place in the larger scheme
of our life. This is mainly because we actually don't know which of
our "personal wins" will be the one that causes the biggest and most
amazing change in our lives. While this card is around, celebrate all
of your achievements. Revel in even the smallest victory. Keep the
energy of success moving.

The Six of Cups can make you nostalgic for the so-called good old days. However, be warned, as your memory is not to be trusted. For whatever reason, memories all come with a bit of a rose-colored hue to them. We romance about things that have been lost and allow ourselves to reminisce on memories of events that weren't actually that great. The Six of Cups can put us in the trap of comparison, making us believe that the life we have already lived is somehow better than the life we are currently living, and that if only we could go back, things would be better again. Alas, this is never the case, and wallowing in the past never creates anything positive in the future. The only time looking behind is helpful is when we are looking for patterns of behavior we wish to eradicate. Self-sabotage and its triggers are important pieces of data to have, so if you must get swept up in this card, look for the ties that bind you to repeating cycles. Start cutting away at the ones that no longer serve you. Offer them up for healing and use the flowing waters of the cups to cleanse your wounds. Now fill the empty spaces with love and light and bring yourself back into the present moment, because you can only create from where you now are, not from where you have been. It is what you feel, think, believe, and do in this moment that shapes the world in which your future self will live. The past no longer exists, so release it.

The Six of Pentacles shows us both sides of the coin, for it could be you in the act of giving or it could be you allowing and receiving. There is even a chance you are in the flow of both, gathering your blessings in one hand and sharing blessings with the other. In many respects, the Six of Pentacles is about the balance one needs when it comes to receptive and blessed energy. The world is a better place when we are all in the flow of health and abundance. When we are blessed, it feels only right to bless someone in return. This is not about giving away what we have received, however. If everything that came in suddenly went back out, we would be missing the whole point of this card. This is about balance, about weighing that which you have and need against that which you can share and pass on. This can be done in so many ways. Time, knowledge, and money are just a few examples. This is why we see scales on many versions of this card, for there is a fine line between giving to your own detriment and giving as a way of bringing more abundance to you. Not everyone knows where that line is, which is why the Six of Pentacles is here to assist. There is a nice, gentle grounding energy about this card, which allows you to take your time and to get into the swing of a new habit. There is no rush to get this balance right the first time, and the scales allow for trial and error without judgment and ridicule. Take your time and ease into the energy that this card offers up around your material being.

PATHWORK

Intentional

If you have made it this far through each of the suits, then you have experienced some change and growth since you started back in the Aces. The Sixes are linked to the Lovers in the major arcana, and they are just as much about commitment as their more celebrated major card companion. The change you experienced in the Fives is now asking you to shore up your commitment, to take the next step as the new person you are creating, to journey into the unknown of the path you have now cleared, and to only bring the lessons and love from the past that you have left behind. In many respects, the Sixes can be difficult cards to navigate, as they are not as clear-cut as they seem. The middle can be mundane, messy, and often tedious, but you can't just skip to the end without traveling the middle first. Let's see where exactly you are on your journey and take a look at what you need to reconfirm and what you need to recommit to. Pull the four Sixes out of your deck and place them faceup in front of you. Take a good long look at the cards and select the one you are the least drawn to, the one that in some respects repels you. This card represents the part of your current journey that you need to work with, while you are in this middle ground. It is not something you want to wait until you get to the end to deal with, because if you do that you will surely self-sabotage. So, what is it you need to work on while you move through the middle lands of the minor arcana? Think about how this card stands between you and your commitment to reaching the end of your journey and seeing your dream seed manifest. What do you need to do to make sure you can move on without any lingering doubt, guilt, or shame? Use this card as your meditation focal point for the next couple of days. Consider pairing it with the Lovers card as a point of healing, and by all means journal with this card as much as possible.

Intuitive

Sometimes we have to be different people at different stages of our journeys. Most people already understand that who they are at the beginning of something is not who they are at the end, but what about the middle? You need to take another look at what is going on from the new perspective of who you are now, this middle you. To do this, remove all sixteen court cards from your deck, give them a little shuffle, and lay them facedown in front of you. Go ahead and intuitively pick one, but leave it facedown for the time being. Now remove the four Sixes from your deck and place them facedown in front of you, shuffling them around. Go ahead and intuitively pick one. Turn both your selected court card and your Six card over, so now you can see what they are. The court card represents who you are right now, such as the personality, gifts, and blessings that you bring to the middle of your journey. The Six you turned over shows what issues this new you needs to be attending to. I suggest you sit with these cards for a while and really take in the images, as the cards themselves always have a story to tell. Notice how each card makes you feel. Notice if they share colors, shapes, designs, or even suits. Did you select one of them in the reverse aspect? If so, keep it that way; it is important to the overall lesson and meaning of this middle space you now find yourself in. Gather as much information as you can with your eyes, then close them and just meditate on all that you have seen and felt. Take your time with these two cards, as they may be part of your vibrational orbit for the next few weeks. Feel free to record all of your findings in your journal so you can take a deeper dive into the cards at your own pace.

Wandering

For this exercise, seek out the people who best represent each of the four Sixes. They may not be easy to find, but as you start to look for the personality traits of each card, they will start to stand out all over the place. So what personality traits might you be looking for? For the Six of Pentacles, look for someone who gives willingly, or someone who is always looking for ways to invest their money so that it can grow and be used to assist more people and personal projects. For the Six of Wands, look for people who understand the importance of the small successes in life, such as getting through the day without dropping food on their clothes or just being able to complete one task before they move on to the next. For the Six of Swords, look for people who seem to be on a journey from one version of themselves to another. Last but not least, Six of Cups people are those who know that the past is only as important as the lessons and love it brings into the present moment. They use the past as a tool to move forward now. I suggest you actually sit down with these cards and write up a list of additional personality traits for each individual card. The more you know and understand their personalities, the easier it will be to spot them in the people around you. Identifying these people will help you move closer to your goal. They will help move you along the middle path of your journey. They will show you how to commit to your current journey and help you identify what you are still dragging along behind you from your past. Finding the Sixes in the people around you will help your dream seed grow healthier and stronger.

SEVENS

The Sevens in many respects are ambiguous, with each of these cards seeming to have an "either or" meaning or representation. Just when you think you have a Seven sorted out, it throws up another possibility. I guess this is why the Sevens in numerology are associated with lessons and learning. It could even be said that there is not a lot of action in these cards. We are either distracted and taking a stand, but not actually moving; daydreaming about what will be when our manifestation ripens; or worrying about what we have, what we don't have, and what we think we should have. So what lesson have you come here to learn? Have you wandered into the Sevens to learn how to set boundaries, or have you come here to learn how to refine your feelings and decision-making? Perhaps you have to learn patience. There is no doubt that lessons are many within the Sevens, be they emotional, mental, spiritual, or physical.

The Seven of Swords is the first of our ambiguous cards. Is this the card about stealing or reclaiming? Is the character in the Llewellyn Classic Tarot stealing swords or taking back what is theirs? Are there any indicators in the card itself to even let us know what the truth is of what we are seeing? Considering that the swords are a mental/mind card, could it be the mind clearing out thoughts and beliefs and ideas that are no longer needed? Maybe it's your mind reclaiming boundaries in your thoughts, ideas, and beliefs. This is when the other cards around your Seven of Swords in a reading will help you decide whether something is being lost or something is being retrieved.

So what's up with the swords that get left behind? One of the very interesting elements of this card is that there are things that get left behind. But what are those things, and how do we know what to take or reclaim and what to leave behind? Could it be that we are trying to gather elements of our lost goals or dreams? The Seven of Swords is connected to both the Moon and the High Priestess, which also adds to the mysterious duality of this card. Nothing is quite as it seems, and maybe that is the lesson. Don't trust everything you see or think at this time, because not all of it is illuminated. There may be important things hidden and left out of the light in order for you to make good life-affirming decisions.

The Seven of Wands is our second ambiguous card, because let's face it, can you tell if the person in this card is being attacked or gathering support? Just like the Seven of Swords, the Seven of Wands really is up for personal interpretation. Your emotional triggers will dictate how you interpret the image on this card. You will see it either as supportive or combative. So which is it? Do any of the cards around it in a spread or reading make its meaning even clearer or do they just confuse the matter even more? To be fair, there could be both elements playing out in this card at the same time, for when one takes a personal stand and rallies others to support that stand, there will always be those who are in opposition. In other words, you can't please everyone. You may very well be doing

THE MINOR ARCANA   171

what is right by your personal definition, but that doesn't mean everyone around you will see it that way. In many respects, we see elements of the Strength card here in the Seven of Wands, maybe due to its connection to Leo. It takes courage and strength in order to define our boundaries, even if at times we can't tell if we are defending them or reclaiming them.

The Seven of Cups looks like a hoarder's delight with cups filled to the brim with God only knows what. There seems no rhyme or reason or logic to anything that we find stuffed within the Seven of Cups. Maybe they are filled with fantasies and images, fresh from the imagination, offering up possibilities and opportunities. Perhaps they are nothing more than hoarded collectibles gathering dust and serving no real purpose. Maybe they are treasured memories from important times, important places, and important people. Each of these cups could be anchoring you to a past that feels more real than the current moment you now find yourself in. Remember that the decision you made back in the Sixes has influenced what happens here in the Sevens. If you were able to let go of the past and the nostalgic hook that was wrapped around the Six of Cups, then what you see before you now could be a possibility for a new future, a new journey, and a new experience. If, however, you have clung to those past experiences and those past memories and carried them with you into this moment, then the seventh cup is you just making more space to fill with old memories. None of the cups serve a purpose except to fulfill fantasies of a time that no longer exists. So, which is it? Are you clinging to a time, space, and feeling that no longer exists, or are you daydreaming of the possibilities of this new and exciting journey?

The Seven of Pentacles is often depicted in a garden setting with a tree housing the pentacles. However, are these pentacles ripe and ready for the taking or are they still unattainable and offering only a hint of something that you must wait to receive? I have often heard this card described as the card of harvest, yet we do not actually see anyone taking the pentacles from where they are growing. This often leads me to believe that the fruit of our labor is not yet ready to be harvested at all. Instead, it teases and taunts us with expectation and possible potential. You could think of this card as a window into your own personal garden of manifestation, where you can check how your dreams, goals, and hopes are growing. You can see if there is work to be done in your garden based on the cards that surround the Seven of Pentacles in a reading or a spread. Have you neglected your manifestation garden? Have weeds overtaken all that you were growing and now strangle your creations, or does your garden thrive and prosper? Check the other cards around the Seven of Pentacles to see whether or not you are good at this gardening thing, or whether this is a skill you are going to have to sharpen.

PATHWORK

Intentional

You have made it through the change of the Fives and reset your commitment to your goal or dream in the Sixes. Now it's time for a little course correction. The Sevens of the minor arcana are linked to the Chariot in the major arcana, and even though it doesn't always look like there is a lot of movement in these cards, there really are some very firm decisions about direction being made. As you learned with the Chariot, movement is best when it is done deliberately with a firm, conscious intention behind it. One of these four cards holds the key to your next move, and just like the watery undertows of the Chariot, you are going to have to feel your way through your choice. Remove the four Sevens from your deck and place them facedown in front of you. Give them a little shuffle, just enough so you don't know where each one is. Then pick each card up one at time. Do not look at it; instead hold it to your heart chakra. Take a couple of nice deep breaths and see if there is a connection there. If not, just place it to your left and keep going until you find the card that you "feel" is in sync with the direction you know you need to go. Once you have selected your card, and yes you have to choose one and one only, place it somewhere you can see it and leave it there for a couple of days. Pick it up at least a couple of times during the day and reconnect with it on a heart level. You may close your eyes as you make your heart connection, and see if the card itself has any messages for you. You can also journal about what you see on the card itself, such as the colors, the mood, the environment, and anything else that catches your eye and piques your interest. But most importantly, move in the direction your card suggests.

Intuitive

Go ahead and grab the four Sevens out of your deck and lay them faceup in front of you. Just take your time and really look at the pictures. Forget about the meanings for a minute and just let your eyes roam over the four cards, letting your vision register the colors, shapes, and anything else that just catches their attention. As you roam your eyes over the cards, write down the things that pop out at you. They don't have to be in any sort of order, or in any detail, just jot them down. I am sometimes taken in by the lazy yet longing expression that is often drawn on the face of the person in the Seven of Pentacles cards. My eyes focus on the Seven of Cups trying to make out all the things that are stuffed inside them. What is currently catching your eye and pulling at you? The moment you find yourself seeking or deliberately searching for something in the cards, stop. Check over your notes and have a look at what you have written. What is the one thing in your notes that stands out the most and which card is it on? Zoom in on it, pick up the corresponding card, and examine it further. Literally talk yourself through the item, color, or thing that stood out the most to you. Describe it, name it, claim it, and give it a narrative that is relevant to your current goal or dream. This exercise allows you to connect with the card on its terms and does not rely on an already predetermined meaning. Take your time with this exercise and just allow the card to speak to you both visually and intuitively.

Wandering

The Sevens are linked to movement as well as lessons. Have you ever wandered your way through a lesson or learned something while engaging your body? This is known as kinesthetic learning and is a very effective way to remember details and absorb data. This form of teaching is often used with children and adults who have ADHD, as it grounds the information in a way that the brain recognizes. It is also a very cool hypnosis tool. The idea is simple in that you associate a physical movement with something you are trying to learn. This could be remembering an answer to a math problem by pulling your left ear or tapping the end of your nose to recall a specific task on your to-do list. Funny enough, we all learn some form of information this way.

Before you do anything, you need to decide what piece of information you want to engage with in this physical aspect. Is it a reminder to set boundaries with the Seven of Wands? Is it to check in and see what you feel you have left behind in the Seven of Swords?

Is it a reminder to stop daydreaming and get back to work with the Seven of Cups? Or do you want to learn how to know when your manifestation garden is ripe and ready to harvest with the Seven of Pentacles? The best part about this exercise is that you can make it as fun as you want it to be. Get into the same pose as the figures on your card as you affirm your lesson. For example, stand like the figure in the Seven of Wands, but beat your chest as you say, "I make no apologies for setting clear boundaries to protect myself and all that I am creating." If you do yoga this might feel familiar to you, as oftentimes you are asked to affirm or repeat mantras as you hold specific poses. Now go pick your card, get your body in on the act, and have as much fun as possible learning how to activate, engage, and interact with the lessons of the Sevens.

EIGHTS

After the lessons of the Sevens, we are finally able to take action here in the Eights. This action is what is required as we come closer to seeing the full manifestation of your dream seed. You could say that the action we take here amongst the four Eights will determine how well we will end the growth cycle of our current dream seed. What experiences we choose to create now, after we have traveled through the last seven cards of the minor arcana, will dictate the terms of engagement we will have in the last phases of our current journey. The Eights will stretch and challenge us in a way that we have not experienced since the Fives. You will have to decide while working with these cards if you have what it takes to see your goals, dreams, and commitments through to the end. Remember, you are not at the end of your journey within the suits, but this is your last push, your last chance to finish strong. In many respects, the Eights ask, "How deep are you willing to dig to see the life of your dreams be manifested?" You are so close, but you do still have a choice of how you will experience this final phase of your journey. You can do it willingly through hard work and surrender, or you can suffer through because of your attachment to the way things used to be. The Eights let you know that the choice is and always has been yours to make, regarding what you want to experience within the material and physical world.

The Eight of Swords may be trying to tell you that what you took or reclaimed in the Seven of Swords hasn't exactly worked out the way you thought it was going to. Instead you may now find yourself blindfolded and tied to a stake in the middle of nowhere, with your swords stuck in the ground acting like a barrier—creating a scene that echoes the original Rider-Waite-Smith figure on the Eight of Swords card. Yeah, I bet you didn't see that coming, did you? The good news is that this may not be as bad as it looks. For one, you are not stuck; there is plenty of evidence to suggest that if and when you decide to remove yourself from your sticking place, you can do so freely and without harm. Second, it looks like you might end up with some new Jedi mind tricks by the time you make it to the Nine of Swords, as this card is all about what's going on inside your head. Not being able to see suggests increasing one's intuitive or inner sight to solve a problem or find a solution that could not be found or seen before, and this is a true Jedi mind craft. Third, are all of the swords sticking into the ground keeping you in or keeping others out? Either way, I reckon they are doing a sucky job. Just look at the huge gaps between them. They wouldn't stop an elephant! However, I am guessing there very well might have been an easier way to level up your awareness and tap into your superhero mind skills without having to be tied to a stake; unless, of course, you are super stubborn or super kinky and enjoy your lessons hard and harsh. I, for, one am over having to learn things the hard way, but to each their own. Let's hope this time you got the message loud and clear, and you have cleared the path so that what comes next doesn't have to be quite so abrasive.

The Eight of Wands makes me want to duck for cover. To be honest, when I first started with tarot, I honestly thought that the Eight of Wands was an attack card. That those eight fiery wands were coming to rain hell and brimstone down on me. I mean, take a look at most representations of this card and tell me that is not an unreasonable assumption to make. It wasn't until I started serious study with the cards that I learned that this card was actually the opposite of what I thought it was. Perception really is everything. This card is not about blocking or stopping you from moving forward; it is about a burst of energy that has cleared the path for you to move with ease and grace. It is one of the first times we have seen all of the magic wands move willingly in our favor, to be honest. Therefore, it can be both overwhelming and sometimes hard to believe, which might cause you to become momentarily paralyzed. When it has been hard to forge ahead, or you are used to having road blocks and obstacles in your way, it can be slightly unbelievable to see things just fall into place and open up before you. Where there were once walls are now open roads. There is an element of speed associated with this card, meaning that the space that the wands have magically opened up for you won't last long, and seeing as you have no way of knowing exactly how long this gap will be open to you, you'd better not stand around gaping for too long. Magic, fire, and speed flying through the sky? No wonder one can feel as if they are being attacked.

The Eight of Cups will test your remaining attachments, hooks, and emotional triggers. Whatever you didn't deal with or refused to let go of back in the Sevens is now getting all up in your grill. Like it or not, this time you don't have a choice. You have to let go of old outdated ways of doing and feeling once and for all. But let's be honest—did you really believe that you would be able to embrace your new life while you were still holding on to your old life with both hands? Walking away from what you have built in the past is not only necessary, but liberating. Just because you invested time, energy, and money into something doesn't mean it will serve you forever. The Eight of Cups teaches us to move on and admit when something did not work out. This is key in allowing success into your life, for you have to know when to walk away from one thing in order to begin something else. Goals fail, plans fall apart, and people leave. This is a necessary part of your journey here in the temporary world of material things, and the Eight of Cups is here to guide you from what was to what might be. This card might show up to guide you from a course of action that is out of alignment with your heart's desire. It could also be the warning bell you need that your dream seed needs to be moved in a totally different direction in order to fully bloom. All you have to do is say goodbye and find another path.

The Eight of Pentacles is where you get to pound out all of your pent-up frustration. Ha! This is how I often see this card, banging away and working out all of those issues you have had while working your ass off to meet a deadline or achieve a goal. You could say the process of writing this book was me pounding out the Eight of Pentacles on my keyboard. Writing is also a skill, and it is one that takes time to refine. This refinement of one's craft is also an element of the Eight of Pentacles. Although there is a level of expertise that is hinted at with this card, it is a reminder that we must always keep sharpening our skills, and that our gifts and natural talents will always need to be utilized, expanded, and fostered. The more we work on improving our skill set, the more we honor our talents. Just make sure you don't fall into the traps the ego has set along the way, like getting a big head or thinking your gift makes you somehow better than others. For at this stage of the game, you have been noticed, or, more to the point, your talents have been noticed. It might be easy to allow the praise of others to make you think you have learned all you need to learn, but this would be a mistake. Stop pushing yourself now and you will never truly unlock the magic that lies in your gift. You might think you are good; you may even have cause to embrace the appreciation and praise of those around you, but you have not finished your journey. You still have much to learn, and only those who stick to their path and honor their skills will get to see the true blessings of who they are.

PATHWORK

Intentional

In the Sevens you had to think about direction and its consequences and lessons of movement, but now it's time to get it together and tap into the energy of the Strength card so you can finally make it into the last stretch of your journey. The Eights deal primarily with the physical world, the world outside of you. Each of these cards illustrates something you have to do and an actual action step that you are required to take. It could be to finally walk away from all things that no longer align to the person and life you are creating (the Eight of Cups). Or you may need to buckle down and work, work, work (the Eight of Pentacles)! Perhaps it is time for you to take massive action without thinking, and to just risk it all and do it (Eight of Wands). Or are you still trying to create a new life with old ways of doing and thinking (Eight of Swords)? Pull the four Eights out of your deck and place them faceup in front of you. Which one of these images calls to you? You will know which one it is because you won't be able to stop looking at it. Once you and your card have bonded, put the other three cards away. This card is your action card; it is the step you need to take to move your dream or goal closer to the finish line. You don't need to sit around and meditate on this; just go do it.

Intuitive

For this exercise, go ahead and remove the four Eights from your deck and place them faceup in front of you. Now turn them all upside down and line them up in the following order: swords, wands, cups, pentacles. Grab a notepad and a pen and start taking note of anything in particular that stands out in the cards. Is it a visual line that now appears across the top of the card, which was originally the bottom? What about the people or figures in the cards? Is there anything about them that jumps out at you now that they are upside down? Are there things about the cards that you never noticed before while they were right side up? Oftentimes reversed cards act like a mirror, showing us things that maybe we did not notice before, or showing us things that might feel the same, but are slightly different. As you write down the items that stand out to you, start thinking about how they might have some sort of meaning to your current situation. Perhaps out of your notes you can come up with a mantra or affirmation that you can use when you know you need to act but are struggling with fears and doubts. Take your time with this exercise and really study the line of cards in their upside-down state. You just never know what sort of "aha" moment you might have now that you have shifted your perspective.

Wandering

As you move into this final leg of your dream seed's journey, you will find that you will enter all four of the Eights at some point while you make your way to the Nines. You might lose some friends, or find it's time to step away from a job, or even a client. Walking away from one thing is always required when you are walking toward another. You might find yourself putting extra hours in on your project now that it has real momentum. Your world has changed as you have journeyed through the cards, which means you have changed too. Keep this in mind as you wander today, as you may find yourself walking with one or more of the Eights. As you navigate the Eights, watch as they present themselves in your day, notice if you had to walk away from something, if something just lined up perfectly, if you found yourself having to use skills or tools you have never used before, or if your day was filled with people wanting your services and throwing money your way. Your success vortex is in full swing, but you must wander with awareness to see the opportunities the Eights have waiting for you along the path.

NINES

The Nines in numerology mark the end of a cycle, a point of karmic completion, if you will. It is in the Nines that we are transformed into more mature and knowledgeable spiritual beings, less concerned with material existence and more concerned with what happens once we leave the physical skin behind. In the tarot, however, we still have one more set of cards to go, which is the Tens. The Nines show you the finish line, though you won't cross it until after you pass through the Tens. This does not mean you have not learned what you set out to learn or achieved what you set out to achieve back in the Aces. There is no doubt that you have grown since you left the Aces, and that you have learned new ways of being, doing, thinking, and feeling. You may have even started to implement these new skills or habits into your daily life. Here in the

Nines, you are seeing what the long-term consequences of your actions will look like. There is no going back from this point, just the ending of what you started. How does your ending look? Is it everything you hoped it would be? What do you need to do here in the Nines to refine it even more? The Nines are not the ending of the suits; this is important to remember, since you can still change how this all ends. You still have one last chance to mold your experience into something worth celebrating. Keep your eyes firmly fixed on the finish line and see yourself crossing it with power, strength, and confidence. Know that you have all the skills you need to make the results worthy of the journey that you have undertaken to achieve them. Lastly, enjoy this final stage, because just like beginning, you only finish a journey once. You will never take this particular journey again. It is unique, and so too will its ending be. Therefore, revel in all that you have created, including the good, the bad, and the indifferent. For once you cross the finish line, it all goes back into the realm of memory and ghosts.

The Nine of Swords isn't exactly the most pleasant of cards to be receiving at this point in your journey, but it does make sense. When things are winding down and coming to an end, it can be stressful, even if the ending is positive. There are always loose ends to tie up and massive amounts of work involved in completing a project. Sometimes even when you think something is close to being finished, you find something more to do. This is a headache and can quite honestly keep you up at night. I know what it is like to have endless to-do lists playing through my head at 2 a.m. Every time this card comes up I find that something literally comes up to interfere with my ability to sleep or relax. It's like a chattering mind, constantly reminding you of all the things you still have to do. This card can be both empowering and debilitating, and it depends on whether you resist it or work with it. I have found the energy of the

Nine of Swords can be very productive if you lean into it and just go with the flow. Leaning into this card could mean getting up at 2 a.m. to do tasks that your mind won't shut up about, even small, quiet tasks that just need to be emptied from your head, then going back to bed and starting all over again when the mind next wakes you up. The Nine of Swords only gets worse the more you resist it, so make a choice. Either harness this energy and use it to make you more productive, or fight it and let it derail you from all the hard work you have done up until this point. It is your choice, after all.

The Nine of Wands could be called the last stand, for it often shows a figure who is somewhat beaten up, yet still on their feet. This again only adds to my initial reaction to the Eight of Wands as fire and brimstone raining down on those below. I mean take a look at the original Rider-Waite-Smith version of this card, or any deck inspired by the original. Doesn't this figure look like he or she may have only just survived eight flaming wands falling from the sky? If you were raised Catholic like I was, you may have very different views of the suit of wands than other people. I am here to tell you that it is perfectly fine and I am right there with you. However, even though the figure in this card does look a little worse for wear, there is an energy about them, a vibe of not being easily defeated, and that despite it all, they are still standing, albeit with the help of that ninth wand, but they are upright all the same. This card could very well be the triumph of the human spirit, meaning that no matter how many times it gets knocked down, pushed around, or kicked about, it still keeps getting back up for more. This is the card that says there is no such thing as failure, and that no matter what tests, lessons, or challenges come our way, we will get through them one way or the other. Standing there with your wall of Eight of Wands behind you, you know what it means to be tested. You have the battle scars to prove how strong you are, and you are not letting anyone or anything stop you from making it across the finish line. If you ever want to dig deep for that last push, then the Nine of Wands is the rallying card you need in your life, because no matter what your outside world looks like, if you have the ability to get back up and keep going, you can achieve anything and everything your heart desires.

The Nine of Cups can be seen as a card of celebration, like someone is about to throw a celebratory party before they have even finished what they started. It might be easy to think that you can take your foot off the accelerator for a while, and that all you have to do from this point on is coast over the finish line, but I urge you to reconsider. No matter how tempting it might be to let your hair down and allow yourself a moment of relaxation, just know it might be the worst thing you could do. It could cause you to lose momentum and make the final lap of your journey that much harder. There is nothing wrong with acknowledging how well you have done thus far, and even sharing some extra time with friends, but don't overindulge and lose your focus; there is still much to be done before you can put this all behind you once and for all. There is another element of this card that needs to be considered as well, and that is this: What if the figure in the card is not actually offering you a drink but instead is asking you what you wish to happen from this point on? There is an element of genie magic around this card, which is just another reason to be slightly cautious, as everyone knows that wishes come with unforeseen consequences. It might be tempting to wish the last piece of your journey away and just find yourself at the end result, but then again, you won't have much of a say in how that end result looks and you will be at the mercy of your wish. Wishes are tricky, slippery things that never quite end up the way we think they will. I guess that is why I tend to see this card as a card of temptation, or as the last stand of the ego to entice you back into the fold. I see it as the card that dares you to stop where you are and forget finishing what you started. I suggest you just say "Thanks but no thanks" and keep moving.

The Nine of Pentacles makes it look like you have reached the manifestation garden of your dreams. Pentacles are aplenty and they glitter and sparkle as the sun dances across their reflective surfaces. It seems like you have stumbled into paradise, but might I suggest you proceed with caution? Remember the Nines are not the finish line, even though they feel like they should be. All of that karmic completion energy just oozes off of them, and it can be very alluring to think that you have made it to your final destination. By the looks of the Nine of Pentacles, it seems like a fine place to stop. However, just like all of the Nine cards, things may not be what they seem here. There is even a possibility that you aren't even in the garden of luxury yet but merely standing at the edges of the outer entrance. The figure you see before you could be nothing more than a gatekeeper wanting to know what price you will pay to enter this unknown garden. And let's face it, if this is only the entrance, how do you know what it looks like inside? It can be easy to get caught up by all the bling this card brings. In many respects, it shows the traps we fall into within the material world. We often mistake a beautiful experience with something that is just visually stunning. We confuse the art of looking with the art of being. We allow ourselves to get caught up in shiny status symbols that are void of any true joy. Suffering may be the only thing we will find when we allow ourselves to be swept up in the illusion of the material world. All that glitters is not gold, and this scene is no different. By all means, take in the sights and soak up the beauty that surrounds you, but stay separate from it and keep on moving to your true joy, your divine abundance, and your eternal health and well-being.

PATHWORK

Intentional

Coming to the end of a journey is always fraught with excitement because the finish line is in sight; dread because there is still so much to do and the finish line is in sight; and exhaustion because, well, the finish line is in sight! Knowing that our time is running out on a certain project or goal fills our body with mixed emotions. Take the Nines out of your deck and choose your card deliberately and intentionally. Which of the Nines sets the best coming to an end tone for your current journey and will keep you on your toes and make sure you finish completely, efficiently, and wholeheartedly? Take a photo of the card you end up selecting and use it as the lock screen of your phone. This is something you will look at repeatedly every day for the next few weeks as you wrap things up, get things organized, and begin your march to the finish line of your goal, dream, or project. Each time you see the image, say this mantra: "I complete my journey/goal with intention and focus, and I am surrounding the finish line with joy and love." Finish with purpose and move into the Tens with power and authority.

Intuitive

For this exercise, have the four Nines in front of you, faceup and in the following order: the Nine of Swords, the Nine of Wands, the Nine of Cups, the Nine of Pentacles. As we move through this exercise, hold each one of the cards in your hand and speak directly to it, starting with the Nine of Swords and ending with the Nine of Pentacles.

You can do this meditation by just reading through it, or, if you prefer, close your eyes and focus on breathwork. By all means, record it and play it back to yourself, or memorize it before you sit down to meditate.

Let us begin. Say the following aloud:

> I bless the Nine of Swords for reminding me that I am not focused on the present moment. That my mind is being haunted by things that have happened in the past or things that have not even happened.
>
> I bless the Nine of Wands for it will assist me in guarding my mind. It will show me how to build better defenses so I can stay firmly rooted in the present moment, as I know what is right in front of me is where my mind and heart need to be focused.
>
> I bless the Nine of Cups for the joyful reminder that here in this moment, in this space, all I could ever want is already provided. I know that what is in my heart is being manifested and I am allowing myself to feel the joy of the experience as I now step into it.
>
> I bless the Nine of Pentacles for showing me what is possible. For sitting with me during every visualization session and for wrapping me in its abundant energy long enough to bring this current moment forth.
>
> The Nines of the tarot have blessed and guided me while showing me how to take another step closer to my soul's potential. I am filled with gratitude for this gift. I bless these cards. And so it is.

Wandering

This exercise is somewhat tied into the intentional pathwork section, for as you are constantly reminding yourself about how to wrap things up while you head toward the finish line, this exercise wants you to be on the lookout for that card in your daily wanderings. Everything that you think, feel, and do from this point on is being influenced by the card on your phone, the one you deliberately selected, so be on the lookout for it. Listen carefully so you don't miss it when it speaks to you through other people. Watch the actions of those around you and notice if they indicate anything you might have missed as you make your way toward the finish line. The wandering exercise is actually one of the best ways to identify and navigate blocks and self-sabotaging triggers, because you are actually moving and negotiating your way around an idea, concept, or point of meditation. Nowhere is that more important than when you are getting ready to wrap something up and close the doors on an experience as it comes to an end.

TENS

Welcome to your last stop in the numbered cards of the minor arcana. You have made the journey from Aces to Tens, while learning some things about yourself along the way. Unlike the karmic completion you reaped the benefits of back in the Nines, here in the Tens you have physical completion. In truth, ten is really a starting point, for in numerology the number ten would be considered arriving back at another one. This means that here in the last numbered card of the suits, you not only get to see how you have finished your walk through the four elements, but you also get a glimpse of what is to come. Think of it this way: by ending with a specific energy or vibration here in the numbered cards, you set the tone for your next experience or point of expansion. I guess you could say that how well you end this part of your journey will dictate how good a start you have for what is about to come. This gives the Tens a bit of prophetic quality to them. However, like all things that have yet to happen, they are not set in stone and can be altered or changed depending on what thoughts, feelings, and actions you take once you leave the Tens behind you.

This is food for thought as you make your way through these remaining four cards. How did it all end for you? Did you get the results you were hoping for? Did it all end up being too much for you and you just gave up? Does knowing that each of these four cards will set the scene for what comes next change how you see them and what course of action you will take from this point on? Be mindful as each of the cards offers up their lessons to you. Seek both the blessings and the challenges in all four of these remaining cards, and keep your mind open to the opportunity each of these cards presents. These things can be easy to miss when you finally cross the finish line of a journey. You focus on the act of completion, as you should, but far too often miss the real gift of the journey, the seeds of potential that only ending one cycle could produce.

The Ten of Swords is the ultimate "it's over" card. There is no coming back from the ending that has played out in this card. Once you have been slain by Ten of Swords and find yourself facedown in a ditch, maybe it is best to consider staying there for a while. Obviously what you have been doing is not what you can continue to do, unless of course you love being stabbed in the back over and over again. Which, you know, is fine if that is your thing, but I would recommend thinking about taking a completely different approach once you have pulled all of those swords out of your back. I don't say this very often, but this is one of those cards you can't ignore and hope it will go away. When the Ten of Swords shows up, like it or not, the object of your question is done, finished, complete, never to happen again, or at least not in its current form. This is why the details matter. In its current form, this situation, person, or idea is dead in the water; however, that doesn't mean something else won't work. I have seen this card present itself when I have been working through creative ideas for books and decks, and every time it shows up, I know I need to scrap the idea and move on. Damn if this card isn't always right! Therefore, take heart, because even though what you have been doing is over, it does not mean that all is lost. It just means you have to think of a different way to approach your goal, idea, or situation.

The Ten of Wands isn't having a very good day. Like the Ten of Swords, the only happy ending you are getting here is the one you will have once you find somewhere to dump all of those damn wands. I call this card the "screw this shit" card, because that is often how people are feeling when it shows up in a reading. After being beaten up and standing for hours on end for no real reason in the Nine of Wands, you might be thinking to yourself that this is all just a huge waste of your time and you would be so much better off packing it in and going home. You might be absolutely right. Sometimes the best way to move forward is to retreat and regroup, which is one of the better ways to look at this card. You did your best, you got knocked down a lot, but you're still standing, so take the small win and go home and heal. Playing with all of that fire is bound to leave you with some scars, so you might want to get those attended to before you consider your next move. The Ten of Wands will ultimately be your breakdown or breakthrough card, depending on how you see the act of retreating. I, for one, am all for taking a step back and regrouping, as nothing is ever gained by trying to force something into being through exhaustion and sheer will. We all hit a wall while working on our goals. If we didn't, something would be terribly wrong. This is your wall, and you just happen to hit it right at the end. But that does not mean that all is lost, or that you traveled this far in vain. It just means that there is going to be more work to do. This is your seed, lesson, and blessing from the Ten of Wands card. You can either take it and go tend to it lovingly while you rest your mind and heal your body, or you can curse at the universe and never pick the seed up, choosing to end with anger and frustration. Just know that how you end is how you will begin. Choose wisely.

The Ten of Cups is the happily ever after card you never knew you wanted. I say this because there is an element of romance about this card, as if this particular ending is being seen through rose-tinted glasses. This is not to say that things aren't happy or that your ending was not better than you thought it was going to be; it is just a small warning to not get too caught up in how it looks. Looks, as we have learned in our journey through the minor arcana, can be deceptive, which is why it might be best to check in with how you feel. This is a cups card after all. How you feel right now in this moment will be the real indicator of how successfully you have completed this particular cycle. There is a certain amount of euphoria when one completes a big goal, lands that dream deal, or even snags their heartmate, but it is important to remember that this is a heightened sense of being. In other words, you're high on good vibes, and at some point you are going to come crashing down. This is one of the problems with peak emotional states, be they good or bad. They never last longer than the moment that created them, and this causes problems in the moving on process. When things seem too good to be true and make you feel blissed out, you can spend the rest of your life trying to recapture that high, or in this case to replicate the scene being played out in the Ten of Cups. Celebrate, by all means, but don't let this illusion seduce you.

The Ten of Pentacles is often referred to as the legacy card, meaning it is the card that shows the good job you have done with your material and physical resources. However, that might be limiting this card just a little. Sure, it is nice to know we have done so well that those who come after us will benefit from all of our hard work, but there is more to this card than what is left behind after all the work is done. This card represents a level of expertise or a set of skills that has been masterfully refined after thousands of hours of work. This expertise not only helps others, but it also helps you, as doors will now open to you that you never even knew existed. Remember the Tens are seed cards just like the Aces, as they both vibrate to the energy of the number one. The seed offered up by the Ten of Pentacles is different from the seed you planted back in the Ace, for you are no longer a novice; now you are an expert. People, projects, and opportunities flock to you because your name and your work now mean something. You may have started to get recognized back in the Eight of Pentacles, but it is nothing like what can and will happen here in the Ten of Pentacles. The trick with this card is to not let this all go to your head. Humility is key at this level. With each new level there will always be a learning curve, so reign in the ego and stay receptive. Don't blow everything you have worked so hard for by allowing the ego to creep in the back door of your mind. Stay grounded and be fully present to this wonderful new opportunity that you have masterfully manifested. You have done well in providing a secure future for those around you. Now go and have fun; do all the things you have always wanted to do.

PATHWORK

Intentional

You have made it to the end of the minor arcana. Congratulations! This means that whatever you planted back in the Aces has come to pass, even though it may not quite look how you imagined it would. There will be one card in the Tens that you hoped you would end on, and then there will be the card that you actually do end on. What we hope will happen usually differs greatly from what actually does happen. So, which card visually shows your ending? I understand that once a goal has been achieved, there is a mixture of all four of these cards present in the heart and mind of the person who now stands at the finish line, but for this exercise just select one of the cards. Choose the one that best represents how you feel and think as you end this journey. Really study the image on the card. Look closely at what is happening in the image. Notice the colors, the shapes, and the way your eye moves around the image. Let the vibrancy or dullness of the image overtake you, until you and the image seem to be one. Close your eyes if you feel inclined to, and just let the feelings and thoughts that this image brings up flow through you. Do your best not to attach yourself to whatever feelings surface or whatever thoughts slip into your mind; just breathe it all in and breathe it all out. Everything is now over. Hanging on to anything at this point will only bring problems for what comes next. As you let all of these feelings and thoughts flow through you and out of you, say "Thank you" over and over like a mantra. Regardless of where you now find yourself, you have grown, you have experienced change, and like them or not, you have learned new ways of being and doing. Thank the experience for the blessings, gifts, and lessons it has bought into your life. Thank it and release it. Keep your card out for a couple of days, just in case you feel you need to repeat the releasing and gratitude work.

Intuitive

The Tens not only mark an ending, they also mark a beginning. In numerology, the ten is seen as a one, a beginning number. The one connects us to the Magician in the major arcana and lets us know that as we begin a new phase in our lives, we will find that we magically have all that we need. This is where you now stand, at both the finish line and starting line, with a bag full of new magical tricks and tools that you have gathered on the journey you just completed. One of these four Tens is setting the tone for the next vortex of energy that you will step into, but which one is it? Pull the four Tens out of your deck and place them facedown in front of you. Shuffle them around just enough so you don't remember where each of them is, and gently run your fingers over the backs of the four cards. Ask the following question in your mind: What ending is forming my next beginning?

When you notice a sensation in your fingers, be it heat, cold, or tingling, select your card, just the one, and turn it over. So what is it? Which Ten is laying the groundwork for your next phase? I suggest you meditate with this card for a couple of days just so you can go deeper than your initial reaction to it. Let the card dialogue with you through journal work for as long as possible, offering up more information to you. Sometimes we need to really sit with a card before it makes sense or we are able to fully appreciate its deeper wisdom. Take your time, meditate, and don't rush to conclusions about what is starting to form on the horizon of life.

Wandering

I have done many readings with people who refused to acknowledge the finality of the Tens. This level of denial happens to all of us at some point, but over the years I have learned that when a Ten shows up, I had better start looking for the signs of something coming to an end. Now it is your turn to do the same. Something in your life is ending, and something is about to begin. The signs will be all around you, perhaps in the conversations you are having with people, in doors closing, or opportunities disappearing. Know that these endings are meant to be, for you have outgrown the energy and now it is time to move on to a new phase. It is time to expand your awareness to actively seek out endings, and to find an echo of the Tens in the people, words, thoughts, situations, and experiences around you. Let these encounters and interactions guide your decisions and actions so that you can truly harness this completion energy. Timing is everything, so don't hold on to the energy that is now past; instead, release it and let go.

5

· · · · · · · · · · ·

PULLING IT ALL
TOGETHER

IF YOU HAVE MADE it this far through this book, congratulations!
You have done well to make it to the end. But if you have made it
this far, you will also have noticed that the majority of this book is
written with a one-card spread, single card daily draw approach to
it. I admit that was intentional on my behalf, as I wanted to give
you, dear reader, more tools to engage with your cards on a one-on-
one level. That said, I did not really approach the topic of spreads
or how to use this book for multiple-card readings, so now seems
like the perfect time to touch on it and wrap up all that you have
learned thus far in this book.

Let's face it: there is a very good chance you want to know how
to pathwork a reading just as much as you do a single card. So let's
go back to the start of this book for a minute and tap into the three

ways to pathwork your cards: intentional, intuitive, and wandering. For a spread in a reading, I would pick one of these three to focus on. By this I mean you should decide if you want to pathwork your reading intentionally, intuitively, or if you feel you need to physically move the energy that has bubbled up from your spread and wander with your cards. Don't try doing all three for one reading; it will get way too confusing. Just pick one and apply it to your cards. In this way, you are really just finding a more systematic approach to reviewing the information your cards are presenting you with.

Let me give you a quick example. Let's say you have drawn the Nine of Wands, the Ten of Swords, and the Eight of Cups. Clearly something has come to an end and you are being urged to take your battle scars and walk away as quickly and cleanly as possible. You may decide that wandering this spread would be more helpful to your current situation, as each card could help walk you through the steps you need to take to formally complete a cycle, relationship, or job. Here the wandering exercises for each of your cards become small daily actions that keep you moving forward instead of dwelling on what you are leaving behind. Whereas if you had picked the intuitive lens to see these cards through, you might end up entirely in your head and make no forward momentum at all.

Now let's imagine you actively select these cards—you pick them out on purpose faceup from the deck because the artwork just resonates with the results you want to create in your current experience. Then you would read this spread from the intentional section of each card, because everything about your reading is deliberate and strategic. This would apply to any spread you do, regardless of the number of cards. You can do this for client readings as well, though from my own personal experience, you would more than likely use the intuitive or wandering sections as opposed to the intentional. But then again, it depends on how you do your readings with your clients. I would encourage you to take your pathworked spreads to your journal and see what other messages, solutions, action steps, and guidance you can draw out of the information. Let your spreads be roadmaps to your success. Let them show you and your clients how to move out of ordinary and into extraordinary.

You are now ready to embark on your own personal patchwork journey. Use this book as a guide and refer to it whenever you feel stuck or lost. Think of this book as a teacher giving you bits of advice and holding your hand along your pathwork path. I wish you well on your new adventure.

A final note:

I would love to hear about how you use the three different ways to pathwork a spread on social media, so please tag me in your Twitter (@Leeza_Robertson) and Instagram (@Spellspotionsbookstarot) posts. Seeing how others use my books and decks is fascinating to me, as you are all wonderfully creative and imaginative!

To Write to the Author

If you wish to contact the author or would like more information about this book, please write to the author in care of Llewellyn Worldwide Ltd. and we will forward your request. Both the author and publisher appreciate hearing from you and learning of your enjoyment of this book and how it has helped you. Llewellyn Worldwide Ltd. cannot guarantee that every letter written to the author can be answered, but all will be forwarded. Please write to:

Leeza Robertson
℅ Llewellyn Worldwide
2143 Wooddale Drive
Woodbury, MN 55125-2989

Please enclose a self-addressed stamped envelope for reply, or $1.00 to cover costs. If outside the U.S.A., enclose an international postal reply coupon.

Many of Llewellyn's authors have websites with additional information and resources. For more information, please visit our website at http://www.llewellyn.com.

GET MORE AT LLEWELLYN.COM

Visit us online to browse hundreds of our books and decks, plus sign up to receive our e-newsletters and exclusive online offers.

- Free tarot readings • Spell-a-Day • Moon phases
- Recipes, spells, and tips • Blogs • Encyclopedia
- Author interviews, articles, and upcoming events

GET SOCIAL WITH LLEWELLYN

Find us on  🐦 @LlewellynBooks

www.Facebook.com/LlewellynBooks

GET BOOKS AT LLEWELLYN

LLEWELLYN ORDERING INFORMATION

Order online: Visit our website at www.llewellyn.com to select your books and place an order on our secure server.

Order by phone:
- Call toll free within the US at 1-877-NEW-WRLD (1-877-639-9753)
- We accept VISA, MasterCard, American Express, and Discover.

Order by mail:
Send the full price of your order (MN residents add 6.875% sales tax) in US funds plus postage and handling to: Llewellyn Worldwide, 2143 Wooddale Drive, Woodbury, MN 55125-2989

POSTAGE AND HANDLING

STANDARD (US):(Please allow 12 business days)
$30.00 and under, add $6.00.
$30.01 and over, FREE SHIPPING.

CANADA:
We cannot ship to Canada. Please shop your local bookstore or Amazon Canada.

INTERNATIONAL:
Customers pay the actual shipping cost to the final destination, which includes tracking information.

Visit us online for more shipping options. Prices subject to change.

FREE CATALOG!

To order, call
1-877-
NEW-WRLD
ext. 8236
or visit our
website